PSYCHOLOGICAL CARE
IN OLD AGE

PSYCHOLOGICAL CARE IN OLD AGE

Nicholas R. C. Leng
Principal Clinical Psychologist
Royal Hospital and Home
London, England

⬤HEMISPHERE PUBLISHING CORPORATION
A member of the Taylor & Francis Group
New York   Washington   Philadelphia   London

PSYCHOLOGICAL CARE IN OLD AGE

1 2 3 4 5 6 7 8 9   B R B R   9 8 7 6 5 4 3 2 1 0

This book was set in Century by Hemisphere Publishing Corporation. The editors were Lisa A. Warren and Christine P. Landry; the production supervisor was Peggy M. Rote; and the typesetter was Cynthia B. Mynhier. Cover design by Debra Eubanks Riffe.
Printing and binding by Braun-Brumfield Inc.

A CIP catalog record for this book is available from the British Library.

Library of Congress Cataloging-in-Publication Data

Leng, Nicholas R. C.
    Psychological care in old age / Nicholas R. C. Leng. p.   cm.—(Series in death eduction, aging, and health care)
    Includes bibliographical references.
    1. Aged—Mental health. 2. Mentally ill aged—Care. 3. Aged, Physically handicapped—Care. I. Title. II. Series.
    RC451.4.A5L46   89-71072
                                                        CIP

ISBN 1-56032-049-4
ISSN 0275-3510

Contents

8 Death and Bereavement 121

Preface

The idea for writing this book came from two sources: (a) training care staff in the psychological management of elderly patients and (b) attempting to help those relatives looking after an elderly person themselves. The book therefore has a twofold purpose. It is aimed at both the professional and the home caregiver. Most of us will be or will know a close family member who is in the position of caring for an older relative. Such people are faced with trying to cope with what is probably one of the greatest stresses of our time. Often the task falls to one family member alone, more often the wife or daughter, less often the husband. In one case, I encountered a woman who was attempting to look after her mother and her husband simultaneously, both of whom suffered from dementia.

Until recently, little attention has been paid to the disorders more commonly encountered in old age, although in heimer's disease, which, although more usually affecting older people, can strike tragically in the middle years. Now the situation is beginning to change. There is greater public awareness of the fact that there are more elderly people, and there are signs of professional people choosing to work with this group of clients.

Reading the book may give the impression that the assumption is that readers will themselves be elderly and probably female. If that impression is gained, then no apology is offered because this is the position of the "average" home caregiver. Particularly in Chapter 1, the advice given is directed perhaps more toward caregivers who themselves are getting older. Hopefully, however, the book will be of interest to anyone concerned with aging, either as a caregiver or as one who is experiencing old age, or even preparing for it. Most of the book, however, is concerned with the major pitfalls of old age: depression, stroke, dementia, and other conditions. The general approach has been to describe these conditions and then to provide some advice about management. I try to avoid being either too pessimistic or unrealistically optimistic. The aim has been more to try to summarize current psychological knowledge as accurately as possible and in a relevant and practical way. However, I believe that psychological management cannot meaningfully be separated from other aspects of care and that good management involves looking at physical, psychological, environmental, and social factors. For this reason, I discuss certain aspects of basic nursing and physical care, as well as environmental factors that relate to the care of the elderly; readers who seek more detailed information about nursing and medical care will need to consult other books. Suggestions for further reading are given at the end of each chapter.

Nicholas R. C. Leng

1

Growing Older

This chapter differs slightly from those that follow. Its aim is somewhat broader. First, it is aimed at older people who, at least at present, do not need such care but who are interested in learning about the psychology of old age. Second, it is also aimed at caregivers, be they professionals or laypeople, as an introduction or context within which to set the remainder of the book. The rest of this book is concerned with giving advice to those who are looking after older people.

Cicero informed us that although life could be likened to a play, it was one with a rather disappointing last act. The intention here is not to attempt to rewrite this last act, desirable for some though that may be, but to describe its high spots and anticlimaxes and hopefully to show that all need not be lost.

Most people today are aware that the proportion of people over the age of 65, and especially those over the age of 75, is increasing. This is due largely to advances in medical care and social improvements.

We could spend some considerable time trying to define

what old age is. Intuitively, we all recognize it when we see it, but attempting to define it is more difficult. Definitions in terms of chronology are not very helpful because we can all think of "old" 50-years-olds and "young" 70-year-olds. Thus, to say that old age starts at age 65 is quite arbitrary, for there is nothing special about this particular age, or any other age for that matter. Yet, medical and social services for elderly people often start at age 65. This has caused much alarm to many of my patients who have been horrified that, because they are in their late 60s, they must now see a geriatrician, or worse still, a psychogeriatrician. Thankfully, in some areas there is more enlightenment. Some physicians will not adhere strictly to the age cutoff point but will tend to agree to see patients according more to the nature of their problem than simply to their chronological age. Others have refused to call themselves geriatricians or psychogeriatricians and instead call themselves physicians specializing in the care of elderly people. I am sure that such moves are in the right direction, although we have a long way to go yet.

That, then, is the general tone of this chapter and indeed the whole book—that old age is not some kind of abnormal peculiarity. It may have its special tasks, but otherwise we need to remember that we are the same people all throughout our lives. We change gradually, but few of us change dramatically just because we have reached the age of 60 or 65.

It is common to think of life as a series of stages through which people pass, as did Shakespeare in *As You Like It.* But this fractionation of the life span is largely for descriptive purposes. The stages are not clear-cut but occur along a continuum, so that each stage merges gently into the next. There is no exact point at which old age begins, and there is considerable individual variation. Some people seem to age slowly in a sort of linear fashion, whereas others appear to remain static for years and then suddenly show a marked outward change in their appearance. It is as if there were a biological clock within us, but the speed of the ticking varies from one person to another and may vary from one point in time to another.

If asked to make a list of characteristics of old age, no

doubt most of us would produce a list of negative adjectives. This illustrates our stereotyped model of old age, and although not denying many negative things do happen when we get older, we need also to remember that older people have the same basic physical, emotional, intellectual, and social needs as everybody else. They may even have additional ones. This may seem obvious, but it is easily forgotten. For example, anyone who has ever visited a hospital or home for elderly people will have been struck by the frequent lack of intellectual and social stimulation. Even people with senile dementia will respond to some kind of stimulation, and so it is important always to remember to maintain a balance by (a) developing an insight into the deficits of older people and (b) remembering that they have some residual qualities and the same basic needs as all of us.

When considering old age it is useful to think in terms of physical, psychological, and social factors. First, let us consider physical aspects of aging.

PHYSICAL FACTORS

Sensory impairments occur quite frequently in old age. Some 50% of older people suffer from a deterioration in eyesight. Spectacles are worn by people of all ages, so there is probably little additional stigma attached to this. Libraries produce many large-print books; if eyesight is very poor and reading impossible, then it is possible to obtain cassette recordings of many publications.

Hospitals and homes for elderly people are all too often decorated in dark and drab colors, and lighting is poor. Young people would not choose to live in a drab and dreary environment, and I can think of no obvious reason why older people would do so either. Lighting needs to be good and colors light and cheerful. This helps compensate for failing eyesight and improves mood.

Hearing impairments are a little less frequent in older people but can be annoying to all concerned. We may feel that others are greatly inconvenienced by having to talk loudly to us and that we are irritating because we keep having to say "pardon." Hearing aids are not popular with anyone, even if they are small and barely noticeable. They seem to reinforce the presence of the disability and often amplify background noise as well as what we actually want to hear, and this can be annoying. Such aids need to be more directional, so that they can be more accurately aimed toward the source of the sound. However, some are now surprisingly compact and, despite their limitations, their benefits probably outweigh the limitations for most people.

Poor balance can be an embarrassment but does not have to be something to be ashamed of. I know of one elderly man who has made a hobby out of collecting interesting handmade walking sticks. There are so many attractive variations. There are many different kinds of wood, ornate carvings, different shapes, and so on. Many famous people used them in public: Sir Winston Churchill, Sibelius, Dickens, and Franklin Roosevelt. Walking sticks really can look quite distinguished.

Shoes with high-friction soles are discrete. They improve safety and confidence on slippery surfaces. Such observations may seem absurdly obvious, but I make them here because so many people seem to deny old age and try to battle against it as if they were years younger. It is better to work toward trying to accept the situation and approach it as a challenge rather than as a curse. If you move with it and do not resent it, you will adapt much better.

Diet and exercise are, of course, important factors. Unless suffering from a particular medical condition, dietary needs are much the same as at any other age; however, vitamin deficiencies can occur if the diet is not sufficiently comprehensive, such as may occur in people who live alone and cannot see the point in cooking for one. Because exercise may be less, the intake of unrefined carbohydrates (e.g., cereals) is important. There is, of course, no need to give up exercise because of old age. In fact, it is a good idea to continue what you have always done, making the necessary downward adjustments as and when required and avoiding any pain or strain, unless otherwise advised by your doctor. Notice that the emphasis is placed on the concept of "continuity" (Covey, 1981). If you have never exercised then do not suddenly go out and attempt to run a marathon!

PSYCHOLOGICAL FACTORS

Intelligence

Psychologists have concerned themselves for many years with the question of whether intellectual powers decline with old age, but answering that question has proved more difficult than might at first appear. Quite a considerable amount of research has been conducted on intellectual functioning in older people, but the picture is still not very clearcut. Studies comparing an older group of people with a younger one have tended to produce different results from those measuring changes in intelligence within a single group of people tested across time. It has generally been found that older people perform less well on intelligence tests when compared with younger ones; for some time it was thought that aging was characterized by a marked intellectual decline. However, such studies have several problems. For example, many older people will not have had the benefits of education that younger people have had, and the concept of an intelligence test may be quite foreign to them. On the other hand, when the same group of people have been tested across time, intelligence test scores appear to be more stable. The current opinion among most psychologists is that although there is a degree of intellectual decline in old age it is not as great as was once thought, not all types of intellectual function are involved, and there is considerable individual variation. For example, older people are more likely to perform more poorly on tests involving spatial than verbal reasoning powers and in new problem-solving situations. However, skills such as vocabulary and acquired knowledge are more likely to remain stable. In everyday practical terms, therefore, we might expect older people to perform as well as younger people in situations requiring the application of acquired knowledge, but perhaps worse in situations requiring response to new and unfamiliar problems.

Memory

Memory loss is a feature commonly associated with old age. Older people themselves often complain of less efficient memory, but memory test scores do not always confirm this. This is largely because older people are actually referring to everyday memory ability, such as forgetting where they have put something; such failures are not necessarily indicative of serious pathology. Memory tests do not necessarily measure these things either. Furthermore, there are many factors that can adversely affect one's memory. For example, depression, which is not uncommon in old age, can have a significant effect on memory, as can anxiety. Generally speaking, older people tend to perform relatively well on tests of short-term memory, such as being able to remember a telephone number long enough to dial it. Older people often complain of doing less well on tests of long-term memory, which involves learning, storing, and retrieving information. Very long-term memory, or remote memory, is often good, and older people frequently report being able to recall their childhood years better than events that happened yesterday or last week.

In particular, older people have a disproportionate difficulty in recalling something as opposed to recognizing it. For example, we may find that it is relatively more difficult to recall a person's name without any clues, whereas our ability to recognize the name if presented will tend to be better.

Forgetting names is a common occurrence, and being unable to retrieve a name can be very frustrating. Very often we know that we know it but we cannot produce it, indicating that the information is certainly there but difficult to access. Performing a logical search can help, such as going through the alphabet to try to remember which letter the name begins with. On other occasions, however, we are aware that we simply do not have the name in our memory; under these circumstances it is quite often the case that the information was never stored properly in the first place. Thus, when being introduced to a person it is important to pay attention, hear the name correctly, and take time to memorize it. Failing to take the name in to begin with is a common reason for forgetting someone's name.

Another problem is forgetting to do things. It occurs to you that when you go into town you must take your suit to the dry cleaners. However, when you get into town or return you realize you have forgotten it. You could, of course, continually rehearse the thought of taking your suit with you up until the time you actually leave the house, but this is inconvenient. A better alternative is to carry out as much of the memory task as possible at the time the thought occurs to you. So, in this particular example, as soon as it occurs to you that you need to take your suit to the dry cleaner, go and get it and hang it on the door knob. You are less likely to forget it and do not need to keep worrying about it.

Another classic problem is walking into a room and then forgetting what you went in their for. This is very frustrating. It occurs because on your way to the room, you started to think about something else, and this displaced the previous thought from your short-term memory store, which has limited capacity and is of limited duration. The way to cope with this is to ensure that you hold the first thought in your mind until you get into the room and prevent any other intervening thoughts.

There are other ways of remembering to do things. External memory aids are used by all of us. I know that I would be quite lost without my appointment book or if my wife did not remind me that I am supposed to be somewhere! One convenient method is to keep a diary and to get into the habit of using it regularly. Make a list of all the things you have to do the next day and the time and place where they have to be done. Alternatively, have a wipe-clean noteboard in the house and keep notes on it. Alarm clocks can be used to remember to do things at the right time. Set the clock for a time that allows you to get to the dentist punctually or to put the chicken in the oven at the right time. Important ideas sometimes pop up at inconvenient times. Write them down immediately, and if necessary put the note in a prominent place.

With the advent of advanced technology there are now electronic memory aids available. These permit the storage and retrieval of information by means of a small, hand-held microcomputer no larger than the average pocket calculator. There is also a system whereby appointments can be stored and an alarm buzzer can be programmed to remind the user at the appropriate time.

Much of our day is routine, and we tend to do things in a set order. Each step is carried out easily because we have learned that it carries on from the previous one. Thus, much of our behavior, such as driving to work, although being highly complex, is done almost automatically. We do not have to think about each successive step. Because such associations have been so overlearned, as psychologists would say, introducing new stages into the routine can be difficult. For example, older people frequently complain that they forget to take their medication. This is because they have to learn a new association, which in this case might be the association "lunchtime pill." One way to facilitate the learning of the new association would be to keep the pill bottle in a prominent place, such as next to the salt and pepper, so that when the table is set you will tend not to forget to put the medication bottle on the table.

Forgetting where you put things can also be a frustrating experience. One solution is to record the whereabouts of things when you put them away. Obviously this would be extremely tedious for many items, but it could be useful for recording the storage of occasionally used items. So, keep a list of important items and where they are located. For everyday items try to put them away in the same place. The most common items to misplace are things such as pens and spectacles, partly because we put them down somewhere without paying attention at the time, and partly because there are a thousand and one possible places where we might have put them. Try to get into the habit of paying attention when you put an item down and you need not forget where you put it.

Another way of improving memory is to use mnemonics. The ancient Greeks were experts at this because their storage facilities for information were limited and therefore much information had to be memorized. By and large, images and pictures seem easier to recall than words. Faces seem easier than people's names. This can be used to some advantage, as I now demonstrate. Much of the history of these methods is given by Yates (1966).

In 477 BC a poet named Simonides was reciting a poem at a banquet and while he was out of the room, the ceiling collapsed. Many guests were crushed in the accident, but Simonides was able to identify the bodies because he could remember the exact locations where people were seated. He did this using the *loci method*. *Loci* is a grammatical form of *locus*—the Latin for *a place*, which is where the word *location* comes from.

The loci method is quite simple to learn and to use. All that is required is the ability to form a clear mental image of a familiar place. This place can be a room in a house, a whole house, or a large public building. The important thing is that the place is well known to you and that it contains a number of identifiable features so that the whole thing can be clearly visualized in your mind. Having chosen the place that you are going to visualize, the procedure is then to form an image of each of the items you want to remember, whether they are objects or people, in a particular part of the room or house. The images that you form need to be as clear, intense, and unusual as possible. Suppose that you want to use this method to remember a shopping list containing items such as bacon, dog food, eggs, apples, butter, bread, carrots, dishwashing liquid, soap, and coffee. Use a typical room in your house, say the dining room. All you have to do is allocate each item to one part of the room and visualize the item there for a few seconds. For example, the first item, bacon, could be learned by imagining a picture of bacon hanging on the back of the door. The images may sometimes seem a little surrealistic, but this does not matter, especially if it will improve the learning of them. When you want to recall the list, all you need to do is go around the room in your mind the same as before. As you visualize each location in the room, the associated item will come to mind. Try the method for yourself and compare it with trying to rote learn a list of items. You should find that your memory is very much better using the loci method.

A related technique may be referred to as the *chain method*. Again, suppose that you wish to memorize the following items on a shopping list: bread, carrots, eggs, dog food, newspaper, bacon, and deodorant. All that the method involves is to chain the items together by forming a visual image combining each item with the next item on the list. Because the first two items are bread and carrots, it is possible to form an image of a loaf of bread being cut open and carrots falling out. The next item is eggs, so you might imagine a carrot in an egg box. Dog food is then connected with eggs by imagining half a dozen eggs running around the street on a leash. Newspaper is connected to dog food by seeing a dog reading a newspaper. Bacon is connected to newspaper by imagining bacon wrapped up in newspaper. Finally, bacon is connected to deodorant by imagining someone putting bacon under their armpits. Each image is formed and held for a few moments. When recall is required the word *bread* is first recalled, which will bring to mind the image of bread being cut open and a carrot falling out. Recalling the carrot will bring to mind the image of a carrot in an egg box and so on. Try the method out, first by trying to recall a list by rote learning and then with the aid of imagery.

The third main method of this kind is called the *peg method*. Suppose that you want to remember any 10 items. First of all you need to learn a list of "peg" words. For numbers 1 through 10, it is easy because it is simple to find a word rhyming with each number. Thereafter it is difficult, so learning peg words for numbers beyond 10 takes time, but can be done. Once learned this peg list can be used to remember new items of information. The peg words could be as follows: (1) bun, (2) shoe, (3), tree, (4) door, (5) hive, (6) bricks, (7) heaven, (8) plate, (9) wine, and (10) hen. Once learned the next step is to visualize an image linking together each peg word with a new item. Again, take the example of a shopping list: If the first item were bacon, then you would imagine a bun with bacon in it. If the next word were dog food, then you would imagine a shoe with dog food in it, and so on through the list. As with the loci and chain methods, at the time of recall all that is necessary is to run through the peg list in your mind and the associated items will come to mind.

It can be pointed out, though, that making a shopping list would surely be quicker and easier than using visual imagery in the case of the above examples. However, visual imagery can also be used to improve the learning of other types of information, such as people's names. When introduced to people, make sure you have their names and then associate the names in your mind with the aid of a relevant visual image. When you meet them again, try to recall the original image and this will assist you in recalling their names. An example would be the name *Baker*. When the name is presented, picture Mr. Baker in your mind wearing a baker's hat and holding a loaf. Mr. Rose is imagined holding a rose. Frank is imagined holding a frankfurter. Nicholas is imagined dressed in a Santa Clause outfit. Some names are not so readily imagined in this way, but with practice most can be altered in some way so as to be easier to visualize. Thus, Mr. Metcalf can be imagined as shaking hands with a calf. Mr. Freedman can be imagined as a freed man. Visual imagery also allows us to learn associations between people's faces and their jobs or interests. Thus, if Mr. Smith is a good squash player, he can be visualized on a squash court playing with the world champion. With practice the method can be used with some benefit.

Another popular mnemonic is the *PQRST strategy*. *P* stands for preview (i.e., the material is quickly read). *Q* stands for question (i.e., ask yourself key questions about what you are trying to remember). *R* stands for read (i.e., read the information thoroughly). *S* stands for state (i.e., state the answer). *T* stands for test (i.e., test yourself on the answers). This method may be used to improve learning a newspaper article, book, or other related information.

There are several other ways of improving memory, some

of which may be familiar from school days. First-letter mnemonics, for example, have been used to remember the order of battles, kings, and so forth. In chemistry, the order of the elements in the periodic table can be learned by the rhyme "Henry he likes beer, but cannot obtain. . . ," with the first one or two letters of each representing hydrogen, helium, lithium, beryllium, boron, carbon, oxygen, and so on.

All of the above techniques may appear a little daunting and elaborate, but if you take time to practice them, they are likely to help in the learning of new information; your self-esteem will also be enhanced by demonstrating to yourself that you can improve your memory.

I have spent some time on memory because complaints about it are so common in older people, but before ending this section I must consider a few more psychological factors.

Reaction Time

Reaction time simply refers to the time taken for a person to respond to a given stimulus. An example would be the time taken to respond by putting one's foot on the brake pedal when the traffic light turns red. Elderly people do seem to take longer to react to things happening around them; the more complex the situation is, the greater the difference between younger and older people. However, as with intelligence and memory, there is considerable individual variation, and some elderly people have faster reaction times than others. On the average older people are about 20% slower than younger ones. To some extent older people may react more slowly to try to minimize making an error, but it is worth remembering that accuracy and speed are likely to be adversely affected by old age when it comes to many everyday tasks, some allowance should be made for this.

Personality

Most people have stereotyped views about personality in old age. Rebelliousness and a tendency to be outgoing are usually associated with youth, whereas we tend to take the view that as people become older they become more con-servative, less outgoing, more rigid, and more resistant to change. Rigidity is a personality factor that has been studied in some detail in elderly people. Although there does appear to be an association between rigidity and aging, this is not as pronounced as some might believe. Similarly, older people seem to exercise a greater degree of caution. They are thought to be less inclined to take risks or to make guesses unless there is a high probability of these being correct; they also tend not to respond to a given situation rather than risk making a mistake. Introversion tends to increase with age, so older people tend to become more preoccupied with themselves. I examine possible reasons for this later.

Psychological research has suggested that older people fall into one of four basic personality types. Gaber (1983), for ex-ample, found that about 50% of older people might be de-scribed as average, which is to say that they are well adjusted to old age. They are characterized by a tendency to resist change and are more apprehensive than younger people. They may also appear to be less tolerant. Individuals in the second group, accounting for about 20%, may be thought of as being introverted in that they tend to be shy, more iso-lated, and avoid seeking assistance from others. A third group of people, about 10% of older people, have some degree of emotional and personal disturbance and tend to be poorly ad-justed as a result. The remaining 20% or so are notably inde-pendent, well adjusted, and stable. They are to be found as active participants in many community activities.

Having looked at psychological aspects of aging, I now consider social factors.

SOCIAL FACTORS

I noted earlier that older people tend to become more introverted, but it has been suggested that rather than this being a biological process, it is something that occurs as a result of changes within the person's environment. As one retires, as children leave the home, and so on, life tends to place fewer external demands on the person. This process of disengagement leads to less interaction and a reduced involvement with the outside world, with a corresponding increase and preoccupation with the self. Such a process might be exacerbated through development of disability or ill health. Disengagement might therefore be seen as a less desirable process because in most cases, it would appear that older people wish to remain active and involved. They do not wish to be put out to pasture. There exists, however, a body of opinion that although some elderly people may happily disengage, this is not the case for those who would prefer to continue with previous interests and involvements. In fact, when an older person does suddenly stop doing something, it may well be because of depression.

Level of Functioning

Loss is a central feature of the aging years, and adjustment to retirement, relocation, the death of others, loss of role, and infirmity has to occur. It is not surprising to find that older people who become disabled in some way become less satisfied with life. People confined to the house because of walking difficulties, or worse, confined to bed, will obviously have their level of external stimulation curtailed. This, in turn, must increase the chances of them becoming more preoccupied with their disability and so becoming depressed. However, the relation between age and well-being is not entirely straightforward. Although outwardly older people may appear to be functioning at a lower level, their subjective experience may be different. There may have been a gradual reduction in their level of functioning, and together with the ability to face the inevitable loss of functioning in old age, this may lead to better adaptation than one might at first expect. Problems are more likely to occur when older people's level of functioning falls to below that of their peers.

Relocation

Relocation may range from having to move into a bungalow because stairs can no longer be negotiated to a move into residential care. The former instance is not likely to be too traumatic, but it could be if it entailed moving to a new district where there was no existing social network. On the other hand, many, if not most, older people resist a move into residential care, even if it is perceived as being the most sensible thing to do, because it signals the end of independence and the expectation of further deterioration. Although there is considerable individual variation, there is no doubt that health may suffer as a result of a move. Each case has to be considered carefully, but in almost every case it will be a question of trying to attain the right balance. I return to residential care later in this book, but here I can note that it will usually mean at least some loss of independence, although this may be necessary when community support systems are deemed insufficient.

Crucial to relocation is advance preparation. There is little doubt that such preparation will minimize adverse reactions. People who have become very frail mentally, as in those with senile dementia, are less able to prepare in this way because of grossly deficient perception and memory; they are also likely to react more poorly than the more intact individual.

Another factor to be considered is personality. Some elderly people may view residential care as something of a relief because they can now give up worrying about the struggle to care for themselves. Other more self-sufficient types may not see things that way. In general, however, it would seem wise to try to make the correct decision the first time around so that additional moves are minimized.

Retirement

Retirement is a relatively modern phenomenon. Today, however, life expectancy is such that we can anticipate many years beyond the day we officially stop work. The retirement years can in some cases compare with the working years in their length. For example, if someone lives to be 100 years old, as one of my grandmothers almost did, then they could have spent as much time in retirement as they did working!

Many people retire happily and are relieved to give up the daily drudgery of work, especially if they have done boring and repetitive jobs or if there have been changes at work resulting in new demands and stresses.

Others may have had great personal investment in their work and had little time or energy set aside for other things. They may suddenly find themselves high and dry and will need to find new occupations to replace this loss. At a personal level, adaptation to such changes will depend on people's view of themselves, whether they feel confident and have a good level of self-esteem. If not, they may be less likely to experience a smooth adjustment. The more important the job or person has been and the greater the degree of personal involvement, the greater the degree to which the loss is likely to be felt.

Retirement may be looked forward to, and it is common for the early days of this period to be viewed as something akin to a holiday. But after a time this feeling goes, and this is when adjustment problems can occur. There is much more to work than the job itself, even in the most tedious situations. Work provides a very important part of a person's identity. It fills at least a third of our lives, half of our waking lives, and perhaps more if we tended to think about our work outside of working hours. It provides us with financial reward, and organization to our day, maybe fringe benefits for some, and a sense of pride in knowing that we have worthwhile and valuable skills that may have taken years to develop. Work provides an important source of social contact, both in and out of working hours. Work removes the person from the home, and many marital problems come to the fore when the husband is at home all day and the couple are facing each other 24 hours a day for the first time in their married life. The wife may feel an invasion of her privacy, no longer having a period of time to herself, and there may be guilt felt at doing things separately as an attempt to resolve this. Spare time now has to be filled. The newly retired husband may feel at a loss without the need to go to work, and he may start to take things over at home that were once the province of his wife. This can lead to resentment and conflict.

If we accept, as I mentioned earlier, that for most elderly people good adjustment is to be achieved through continuity, then we should expect people to do better if they avoid sudden and radical changes in their life-style, including relocation and sudden and unplanned retirement. The average person may need to gradually withdraw from organized activity, perhaps continuing his or her previous job in a modified form or taking on new and related interests. This bears some resemblance to the football player who, when he stops playing because of his reduced productiveness, becomes a teacher or manager. Where this is not possible, then the retiring person may take a more active role connected with some other life-long interest. The person who always enjoyed going to football games now has the time to become a committee member of the local club. The aspiring gardener can become involved with the local horticultural society. The musician can start up his or her local amateur orchestra. Many may wish to become involved in local political parties or in volunteer activities. If nothing immediately comes to mind, then sit down and take time to compile a list of all the things you like or think you would like doing. Then make a list of all the possible outlets for such interests. Finally, go and get on with it! Of course, in many cases, the experience will be like starting out work all over again—learning new skills, meeting new people, facing new challenges—but this is what life is about, and withdrawing from these life demands is probably not the answer for most.

There are, of course, many things to be done around the house that have been waiting for years. Some might turn to this in horror at the thought of not knowing where to begin! But it is worth giving some examples: decorating, repairs, organizing the garden shed, cleaning out the attic, and clearing out the garage. It is often a good idea to sort everything out and dispose of all things no longer required. Try to make life comfortable. Replace the old bed with a new one, get rid of high shelves, make the living environment easier to live in generally. The home should be made safe and secure—no wires or leads to trip over, awkward staircases to negotiate, or stiff doors and windows to open and close.

The day needs to be scheduled. This may have been easy enough in earlier years when you had to get up to get the children off to school or to go to work, but there may be less demand to do so now. However, a routine is likely to make you feel better and more in control of yourself, so make a plan for the day and stick to it.

Leisure is as important now as before. Keep or start new hobbies—golf, gardening, cycling, stamp collecting, music, reading, amateur dramatics, fishing, walking, or whatever else catches your fancy—and allocate a set time to do these things. There is much going on now in the field of adult education that allows you to join art classes, learn a language, and many more things. A patient of mine decided to study for a university degree in German language and literature, and she did marvelously!

Socializing

It is quite likely that in many cases, just as we become less physically agile, our social skills lose their sharpness. We may become a little less acutely aware of the effect that we have on others. A common cause of friction between elderly parent and grown-up child results from the parent advising the grown-up offspring when this has not been directly asked for. This can be construed as interference by the son or daughter, even though the intentions by the parent were thought to be helpful. The converse may also occur, and the older relative may feel rejected or that he or she is a nuisance, unwanted, or burdensome. On both sides, time has to be taken to reflect on words and actions before they are said and done to try to avoid this happening. As with any other kind of relationship, it is important to prevent disagreements from going too far, and to do so requires work and commitment by both parties. Good relationships are likely to flourish if positive exchanges between partners take place and if negative ones are avoided. This applies not just to family relationships but to friendships as well. The golf or bridge partner who gets let down once too often because you cancel a game because you do not happen to feel on top of the world eventually gives up asking.

I have already mentioned hearing and eyesight difficulties in passing, but these too can have a bearing on your relationships. Because you do not like wearing your hearing aid, or you refuse to concede that you have a hearing difficulty, you turn it off or refuse to wear it and sit in silence instead because you cannot follow the conversation. It is far better to persevere with its use and try to see the funny side of it. People are more likely to speak to you if you listen and take part. Not doing so will be your loss and not theirs.

Mixing with younger people will depend on the circumstances. On some occasions, such as their parties, you might be perceived as being a bit of a bore, so accept this and do not intrude unless invited to do so. On the other hand, there are situations in which your company will be rewarded. I have already noted how much young children welcome the opportunity to play games or have stories read to them by their grandparents. It is important to try to be tolerant of younger people. The world may have seemed a better place when you were young, and today young people may appear to be ruinous, but it is not really so, for if it were, then the deterioration over successive generations would have extinguished the human race centuries ago! The world has indeed changed, and so the demands on the young are different in each generation, but this must not be interpreted for the worse. Every epoch places its own special demands on its productive generation of people. They have to rise to the challenge because older ways of tackling those new demands may not work or may be inappropriate. Every age has its advantages and its disadvantages. The generation now entering its seventh decade may feel that their heyday was more secure, less stressful, more rational, and more predictable than today. But they suffered two world wars and a great depression. The present generation has seen impressive advances in technology, medicine, and social aspects of life. But they have to learn to live with the fears of nuclear energy and the specter of environmental pollution. It is not that one age or the other was necessarily any better. Indeed, they may not even be comparable, but that every age poses its own unique set of problems.

Try to be sensitive about the effect you have on others. Try not to be a bore, keep to the point, and be concise. You will find younger people getting irritated when it takes you 10 minutes of irrelevant rambling to get to the point. Try to avoid being too critical—you have at least as many faults as the next person. Repetitiveness can be unpopular too, for obvious reasons. Be prepared to be told to shut up if you have told the same person the same joke for the fourth time, especially when it was not funny even the first time. Talking about your illness, disability, or age will be a bore too, especially if it is done repetitively. Learn to be self-critical, to accept criticism from others when it is justified, to modify your behavior in the light of such criticism, and to develop a sense of humor.

Also, try to keep in touch with what is happening around you. We keep up with what is going on in the world through many means: newspapers, television, talking to others, and so on. Retirement may mean a reduction in an important source of keeping in touch, so you may need to compensate.

Feelings

We are all subject to experiences that can be pleasant or unpleasant: anger, anxiety, grief, depression, jealousy, and so forth. None of them really disappears just because we are older, but maybe our expectations do.

Feelings of anger may occur. A common source of anger in old age is failure, or rather a sense of subjective failure. We forget an important appointment or birthday, drop something of sentimental value, or fail to live up to our standards in some way. Anger can therefore be prevented by learning to accept that we need to modify our standards. An athlete does not become angry when he or she can no longer keep at his or her peak but goes off gracefully to do something else. So it can be with the older person who must accept a gradual decline and adjust his or her expectations to match performance. Loss of performance in one sphere can be compensated for by developing a residual skill in another. It is very important to develop or maintain a sense of humor. When feeling bad or angry about something, try to see the funny side of it. The best comedians can laugh at themselves, and this is an art that you must learn too.

Jealousy may be seen as a kind of anger and may arise because we resent the ability of someone younger than ourselves. But there have always been people better than ourselves, in every field of human endeavor, so in a sense our age is irrelevant.

Fears are common in old age—fear of dying, falling over, becoming senile, failing, being alone, and so on. Some fears can be alleviated by reassurance. If you have a strange lump or bump, go have it checked. Other fears, such as going out or falling over, can only be overcome by gradually facing the feared situation. Yet other fears may be prevented. If afraid of failing, then set yourself a more realistic target, one that demands something of you but that you have a good chance of reaching.

Other people may fear the effects of aging, such as gray hair, going bald, and wrinkled skin. Of course everyone should look their best, but when people try to look young it very often shows. A wig often looks like a wig because the color never seems right, and the absence of seeing hair actually joined to the head is invariably noticeable. Hair dyes are often in colors that simply do not exist in the natural repertoire. But at the end of the day one says "So what?" People like or dislike you for what you are. They will not cease to like you because you have gone gray or bald. A few wrinkles here and there are far more worrying to you than to others. I know a number of people who have positively improved with aging. On the other hand, those who attempt to cover up what they see as their shortcomings often make matters far worse. If everybody knows you are wearing a wig, then what is the point of wearing it?

Fears about death are common, especially in societies such as our own where the topic is almost taboo and little preparation takes place. In most cases, though, the fear is probably not so much about death itself as it is the act of dying. Everybody would like to go quietly, peacefully, painlessly, and without guilt. It is not always so, and this is what we fear most. The death of someone who was run over by a car at an untimely moment may mean getting to the hospital just in time to say goodbye, but without the time to say the things we needed to say. Of course we are limited in what we can do to prevent such happenings, but we should always ensure that we have made what arrangements we can and that we have left as little undone as possible. Wills should be written, arrangements made, things agreed, and things said and not left in the air. There may be cases in which pain is extreme or the future beyond hope, and no doubt many have genuinely wanted to put an end to their life in anticipation.

ADJUSTMENT THROUGH THE AGES

Finally, having said something about the detailed changes associated with old age, let me end by trying to put it into context. What does old age really *mean*?

There have been many theories of psychological adjustment, although a particularly influential one was proposed by Erikson (1959). Erikson described eight main stages of development, and his model sees the individual's development within a changing society. New demands are placed on the person as he or she develops over the years, with each one leading to an emotional crisis and having to be adapted to in order to produce a new "strength" or "virtue." The task of the individual, then, is to try to adapt to the demands of each stage, and he or she may do so to a greater or lesser degree. Psychological problems are seen to arise from difficulty in gaining the strength or virtue of a particular stage. Failure to adapt to a particular demand at a particular stage does not, however, rule out future adjustment; the individual is able to look back in retrospect at earlier attempts at adaptation. Adaptation is also influenced by cultural factors and not by the individual alone.

The first year of life is concerned with the development of trust, first in the caregiver (mother), and then in oneself through learning to feel confident in the mother's temporary absence.

During the next few years of life, the child becomes mobile and through increasing autonomy has to gradually learn self-control while maintaining self-esteem. A balance between control and freedom has to be reached.

The ages of 6–10 are seen as the "play age," during which children are able to imagine themselves in adult roles. From the age of 10–14, the influence of education is to be seen so that the child learns to adapt to the physical and intellectual demands of the world. At this stage the child may develop feelings of inferiority or inadequacy through having not resolved the preceding demands.

From 14 to 20 is the adolescent crisis, through which one has to establishe a sense of identity and a sense of working toward a future. Failure to resolve this crisis is seen to lead to a maladaptive identification with delinquent groups.

The next period is seen to run from the age of 20 to the mid-30s, and the task is to establish intimate commitments, partnerships, and affiliations. However, care has to be taken not to lose the acquired identity.

The next stage, up to the age of retirement, is primarily concerned with generation. A major task is the guidance of the next generation, and in resolving this stage the individual is seen to have achieved *generativity*. Failure to achieve generativity is considered to lead to stagnation, personal impoverishment, and self-centeredness.

The final task is seen to be the development of *ego-integrity*. This term refers to achieving a satisfaction with one's life and not regretting that it had been something different. This stage of life involves, as it were, putting things into perspective, reviewing one's life, making some sort of sense of it, and integrating the stages into a meaningful whole. Failure to achieve this leads to despair. The person may come to feel disgusted with himself or herself, with others, and with institutions. Each of these eight stages, if successfully resolved, leads to the development of a virtue—

hope, will, purpose, competence, fidelity, love, care, and wisdom, respectively.

In summary, then, the theme of this chapter is that growing old is about continuity and integration. We should not look for sudden and marked changes in our life-style, but instead try to continue using the same strategies that have worked for us all these years, adapting them as needed. And we must attempt to draw everything together, to look back over our lives and see how all of the pieces fit together. We might sometimes think that we would have done it differently, but that is so easy to say with hindsight, and without it we would probably have followed much the same course.

CONCLUSION

In this chapter I have looked at some "normal" aspects of growing older. An exception is dying and bereavement, which have been given their own place at the end of this book. However, because it would be unrealistic to avoid the issue of what can go wrong in old age, the rest of this book is concerned with some of the more common psychological problems associated with aging.

REFERENCES AND FURTHER READING

Birren, J. E., & Schaie, K. W. (Eds). *Handbook of the psychology of aging*. New York: Van Nostrand Reinhold.

Bromley, D. B. *The psychology of human ageing* (2nd ed.). Harmondsworth, England: Penguin Books.

Covey, H. C. (1987). A reconceptualization of continuity theory: Some preliminary thoughts. *Gerontologist, 21*, 628–633.

Erikson, E. (1959). Identity and the life cycle. *Psychological Issues, 1*, 1–171.

Furst, B. (1963). *You can remember.* Chicago: Memory and Concentration studies.

Gaber, L. (1983). Activity/disengagement revisited: Personality types in the aged. *British Journal of Psychiatry, 143*, 490–497.

Yates, F. A. (1966). *The art of memory.* Chicago: University of Chicago Press.

2

Assessment and General Aspects of Care

So far I have looked at adjustment to old age when not too much has gone wrong. In subsequent parts of this book I look at specific types of problems encountered in the care of elderly people. However, before doing this, I consider assessment and some of the more general aspects of care and management of the older person who has some disability, because if the assessment is not carried out well, then the future management plan may not work.

ASSESSMENT

It is common clinical practice today for services to be provided by a team rather than by an individual. This is because the problems presented by elderly people tend to be multiple and no single professional can be an expert in more than one area. For example, a stroke victim may have a partial paralysis, a speech problem, and a memory impairment. Each of these needs to be assessed by someone with expertise in each of those areas. Such a team typically comprises medical, psychological, social, and therapeutic elements, and often the whole team will be coordinated by a case manager. The role of the case manager is to coordinate the assessment and management of the patient. In some health care facilities the patient's family will also be included as team members. They may be involved in the assessment and treatment process.

Each member of the team will start by conducting an assessment of the patient's capabilities within his or her own professional framework. The physician or psychiatrist will undertake a medical assessment. The psychologist will usually conduct a neuropsychological evaluation that involves tests and clinical interviews. In appropriate cases the physiotherapist, occupational therapist, and speech therapist will examine the patient and the social worker will investigate relevant background and social factors. There may be other professionals involved, such as dietician, podiatrist, dentist, and so on, but the composition of the team will depend on the health care facility and the services that it provides.

Each professional writes a report with recommendations, and it is on this basis that the treatment, management, or rehabilitation program is designed. A method used at my hospital is to make lists of the patient's strengths and constraints and to estimate the long-term goal. These strengths and constraints will be composed of any relevant advantage or disadvantage, and they may be medical, psychological, or social. Strengths could therefore include the ability to walk unaided, residual intellectual ability, or sound family support. Examples of constraints would include the opposite or absence of such factors. The long-term goal would be concerned with outcome in terms of where the person is likely to reside in the future, the level of care and support likely to be needed, or both. From that point, the next stage is to set short-term goals. These would typically include goals or targets that could be met, theoretically at least, before the next case discussion meeting. A short-term target might be to treat a bacterial infection, to examine memory functioning, or to increase the range of movement of a limb to a predetermined extent. Such goals should be feasible, but it does not matter if they are not reached within the set time limit. More important is that a goal is set so that the team and the relatives know exactly what is being attempted. An example of such a goal plan is given in Table 1.

The patient's progress can then be monitored at, say, monthly intervals. An example of a subsequent case review of the same patient is given in Table 2.

TABLE 1 Patient Care Plan for a 65-Year-Old Man Admitted for Assessment and Rehabilitation, After Having Suffered a Subarachnoid Hemorrhage (Case A)

Strengths	Constraints	Long-term goal
Bowel control	Poor balance	Residential care
Sound skin	Verbally abusive on occasion	
Almost totally independent	Poor memory	
	Perceptual impairments	
Mobility in wheel chair is good	Urinary incontinence	
Communication is good	Hypertension	
	Painful left knee (15° extension)	

Short-term objectives	Time	Who is responsible
Control blood pressure	1 month	Physician
X-ray and examination of knee	1 month	Physician
Establish urinary continence	1 month	Nurse
Monitor verbal behavior	1 month	Psychologist
Relieve left-knee pain with ice packs	1 month	Physiotherapist
Mobilize left knee and ankle	1 month	Physiotherapist
Improve dynamic and static balance	1 month	Physiotherapist
Increase walking distance	1 month	Physiotherapist
Establish independent living	1 month	Occupational therapist
Improve memory function with diary and computer	1 month	Occupational therapist and psychologist
Improve orientation	1 month	Occupational therapist

TABLE 2   Case Review of Patient (Case A)

Changes since last review

Blood pressure reduced
No pain in knee now; range of movement increased by 12°
Continence training taking place, but there is still some incontinence
Baseline of verbal outbursts collected
Now achieves good sitting balance; gets from sitting to standing with
   frame or support
Walking distance increased from 7 to 30 yards with supervision
Has a group program to achieve initiation of daily living activities
Attends computer sessions to practice memory skills
Keeps a diary to support his memory

New objectives	Time	Who is responsible
Continue continence training	1 month	Nurse
Investigate possible urinary tract infection	1 month	Physician or nurse
Provide diary for orientation training	1 month	Occupational therapist
Observe and record impairments of vision	1 month	Team
Mobilize left ankle	1 month	Physiotherapist
Continue to improve balance	1 month	Physiotherapist
Increase walking distance	1 month	Physiotherapist
Continue memory program	1 month	Occupational therapist and psychologist
Devise behavioral program to modify verbal abuse	1 month	Psychologist and team

From the psychological point of view, in addition to conducting highly specialized neuropsychological tests that are not further discussed here, it is useful to look at behavioral disability. A useful method for doing this that can be used by non-psychologists is the Clifton Assessment Procedures for the Elderly, or CAPE (Pattie & Gilleard, 1979). It consists of two complimentary parts. The first is a cognitive scale. This measures the patient's orientation to time, place, and person; knowledge of simple current information; and mental control, reading, writing, and tracing a spiral maze. The second part is a behavioral scale. This evaluates physical skills such as walking, dressing, and washing, but it also takes into account communication and social behavior. From the scale it is possible to obtain a score that gives a measure of the degree of mental and behavioral impairment and some estimation of the level of support and the likely future level of care. The scale can also be used to monitor progress. There are many other scales of this sort, and many health care facilities have devised their own. Although these scales provide a useful overall measure of the patient's ability to function, members of the team will still need to measure individual skills and functions. For example, if a stroke victim is being taught to walk again, then it will be necessary to measure the distance achieved from session to session.

The assessment and treatment processes can therefore be highly structured and tightly interlinked. This helps to prevent any vagueness, loss of direction, or misunderstanding about what is being aimed for.

GENERAL ASPECTS OF CARE

In the previous section I focused very much on the structure of the assessment, goal-setting, and evaluation process. However, this approach in itself is not complete. It is essentially a core or framework on which the personal care approach may be mounted. One can split the person into a series of constituent parts, assess each part, and treat each part, but therein lies the danger that the concept of the whole individual is lost. It is important that the caregiver (and here I am talking mainly about the professional caregiver) is able to stand back and see the individual person as a whole, to understand his or her individual feelings and views, and to see him or her within his or her overall personal, social, and environmental context. In the remainder of this chapter I address this. In subsequent chapters I return to the importance of this general approach to the particular problem under discussion, and I also look at some more specific management approaches.

The general approach to care, management, and rehabilitation here emphasizes responding to the needs of the elderly person as an individual. This may seem obvious, but it should always be remembered, for it is easy to see a person in terms of one or more symptoms or an illness. An important aspect of this is the need to treat each patient in terms of his or her own particular level of ability rather than applying an overall level of care. This approach requires doing only what is necessary, and not doing too much, to help the older person. Doing too much can, in one sense, be as bad as doing too little, for it may reduce independence and self-esteem. Caring is not synonomous with doing. Rather, caring means doing what is necessary in order to help the person care for himself or herself. This does not necessarily mean that in some circumstances we may not need to do a great deal for the older person but that we should remember that the care needs of the older person will vary from time to time and according to the degree of impairment. We must ensure that the help given is for the older person's benefit and not just to reduce our anxiety or because it is quicker. Life is full of risks, and some elderly people are more "at risk" than others, but that does not necessarily lead to the conclusion that all elderly people should have things done for them or that they should be prevented automatically from doing things in order to prevent that risk.

One may take the following extreme example of a person who is confined to a wheelchair. Most people would assume that the person is in the wheelchair because he or she is paralyzed and unable to walk. However, this is not always the case, and it is not uncommon for an elderly person to be found in a wheelchair because somebody at some point has decided that he or she is at risk of falling. Of course, in some instances that may be so. However, the point remains that there seems little justification for an elderly person being in a wheelchair unless he or she really is at high risk or, of course, cannot walk at all. In some cases, the risk of the occasional fall may be a small price to pay for the chance to walk. Although it may be faster to move a person from one place to another in a wheelchair, it is surely more desirable for the person to walk there, with assistance as necessary, even though this may take longer. One patient I know who suffered a severe stroke is perfectly able to walk unaided for quite some distance but does not spontaneously do so and would happily spend all day in his wheelchair. It would be very easy for a new caregiver or nurse to think that he could not walk at all; it would also be easy to say that there is little point in getting him to walk if he is "happy" being in a wheelchair. However, from a rehabilitation point of view, this must surely be wrong. It must be physically more desirable to have the patient walk, and the independence thus obtained must be psychologically enhancing.

The same thing applies to other behaviors. It is better to make the task simpler for elderly people than to do it for them. It may take longer, but it will help preserve their dignity, self-esteem, and psychological well-being, factors that are surely just as important as any aspect of physical care.

Another common omission made by some caregiving agencies is communication. It is not uncommon to see elderly people moved around and having things done *to* them without any explanation or commentary about what is happening, let alone any agreement from them that they are willing to have that particular thing done. Besides representing a lack of common courtesy, it is also an example of bad care.

When considering older people we need to remember that they will have their own opinions about things. They should be treated as adults and as individuals. They have the same basic rights as the rest of us, and any decision concerning them must always take into consideration their own views and opinions. There may be occasions when elderly people refuse at all costs to go into residential care, even though they are at risk. Placing them there anyway is something that I have witnessed, and it does not solve the problem. In fact, it is guaranteed to make things worse. Many readers may be surprised that such comments are necessary, but experience suggests that older people are not infrequently placed in residential care without due consultation because they are "confused." Confused they may be, and they will certainly be much more confused to find themselves in a strange place without previous discussion or apparent warning! Other readers may be equally alarmed for the opposite reason and may take the view that elderly people are not able to make rational judgments all of the time and that sometimes we must make decisions for them. There are two points to be made about this: First, we should not assume or take for granted that we have such a right. Second, there will be occasions when we must act to protect an older person who is clearly out of touch with reality because of senile dementia and unable to make any rational decision about anything, but we must never assume that an older person is so confused that it really does not matter what happens or how it is carried out. Even confused elderly people will show some response to the environmental context they are in. They will respond better if only to a calm, relaxed voice; an empathic and genuine reassurance; and a warm, physical touch.

In summary, then, elderly people should be treated as individual persons. They have the same basic human needs as everybody else, and sometimes they have additional special needs. However, their views and opinions are as important as their physical care needs, as is their psychological well-being; we must always give these their respective weight in all aspects of care and in every decision, however minor.

Keeping those general points in mind, let me now consider basic aspects of nursing care as they apply to elderly people.

General Physical Aspects of Care

Obviously many illnesses may lead to hospital admission and skilled nursing care. Here I only deal with basic aspects of nursing that can be learned and applied fairly easily when someone becomes ill. Nurses will obviously already know about these things, and this section is directed more toward the home caregiver without professional training.

Elderly people may be being cared for in bed, in which case these basic aspects of nursing care essentially involve making them comfortable. It is important to make sure that the bed is comfortable. Second, it is important to ensure that they feel clean and comfortable. This includes attending to skin, hair, mouth, eyes, ears, nails, and pressure areas. Third, it is necessary to provide whatever help is necessary in getting them comfortable, sitting up, moving from bed to chair, and so on. Fourth, it is important to ensure help is available with medication, toiletting, washing, eating, and so on. There are techniques for lifting that are summarized below, but I recommend that advice and demonstration on such matters are first sought from a nurse or other suitably qualified person.

One lifting technique is for you to stand behind the person and get him or her to keep his or her arms close to his or her body. If the person's arms are weak, then have the person grip his or her weaker wrist with the other hand. Put your arms through the gap between the person's arms and body and lift by gripping the arms as near as possible to the person's wrists.

A second technique is quite useful for lifting someone up from a chair. Stand in front of the person and to one side slightly. One foot should be beside the person and the other in front of his or her knees. Ask the person to lean forward or help him or her to do so, so that his or her shoulder is near to your body. Then lean across the person's back and grasp the person's elbows by putting your fingers underneath him or her. You can prevent the person's body from turning by placing your arm in front of the person's arm that is farther away.

A third technique can also be applied to a sitting person. Stand in the same position as before, but this time grasp the back of the person's belt or waistband with both hands and lift. Alternatively, with a fourth technique, using the same standing position, place your hands under the person's armpits, with your fingers going under from the back to the nearer armpit and from the front to the farther armpit.

The person being nursed may also need to be turned frequently in bed. No lifting is necessary, but the person must always be moved toward you. Movement is done by rolling or sliding. Roll the person onto his or her back and then move him or her to the side of the bed, so that he or she returns to the middle of the bed when turned. In moving the person to the side of the bed, move the head and shoulders first, then the legs and feet, and then the trunk. Stand with feet apart, place the person's arms under him or her and slide him or her to the side of the bed. When the person is on the left side of the bed, roll him or her onto his or her right side in the middle of the bed, attending first to the head and shoulders. Making sure that the right arm is not trapped, cross the left leg over the right and flex the left hip and roll the trunk using the knee and shoulders as levers.

Special care needs to be taken of feet. Older people are often prevented from getting about because of problems with their feet. Podiatrists advise that feet should be washed daily in warm water, dried thoroughly, and dusted with powder. Toenails should be cut straight across at the same length as the toes and filed from the top if too thick. Socks and stockings should not be too tight, and about a ½-inch gap should be available between the end of the longest toe and shoe. They advise that shoes rather than slippers should be worn indoors and that these should have fastenings. Anything tight around the legs or feet should be avoided because it could reduce circulation. It is better to move around rather than to sit for too long, but when sitting swelling of ankles and aching can be minimized by raising the feet. If problems with feet and nails exist, then a podiatrist will be able to give further advice.

Dental care is also important in old age. Teeth are necessary for eating properly, speaking clearly, and, of course, esthetically. When dentures are first worn there may be some embarrassment, and loss of morale and new dentures usually present some discomfort. A dentist or pharmacist may be able to advise about the best way to keep them clean. Remember also that dentures do need to be changed from time to time because the gums tend to shrink.

Immobility can result from several causes. An obvious cause is some problem with the person's feet. Other causes, discussed in later chapters, are stroke and Parkinson's disease. Another cause is arthritis, of which there are two types: rheumatoid arthritis and osteoarthritis. The former involves inflammation of small joints in the body, whereas the latter is due to the wearing away of parts of weight-bearing joints. A general physician or a rheumatologist will be able to diagnose the problem and prescribe pain relief and anti-inflammatory drugs; a physiotherapist may be able to demonstrate exercises to prevent cessation of use making the problem worse. Immobility can also arise from breathing difficulties, which in turn may indicate heart or lung problems. Advice about dealing with immobility, once the cause has been ascertained, can be given by a physiotherapist or occupational therapist; they may also be able to advise about aids that can be installed to help prevent falls that can result from these conditions. Fear that older people living alone can fall can be a source of anxiety for relatives. It may be possible to get around this by getting a friendly neighbor to pop up quickly every day just to check that everything is all right. Alternatively, some sort of arrangement may be made whereby, say, if a neighbor notices that the curtains have not been opened in the morning, then something may be amiss.

However, something may be achieved through trying to minimize the possibility of a fall by ensuring that there are no things around the house that are easy to trip over or slip on. Older people generally walk more confidently on carpeted floors, which obviously provide a softer surface to fall on as well as not being slippery. If mats are in the house, then rubber-backed ones may be less likely to slip, but they sometimes curl at the edge, which makes them easy to trip over. It is advisable to minimize the amount of electrical cords and to try to keep them near the walls.

An occupational therapist will be able to advise about aids such as handrails that can be installed. These may be placed by the bath or lavatory. Make sure that lighting is bright and strategically located. Special cutlery may be obtained for those with restricted manual dexterity. Walking sticks, with or without a tripod on the end, may be useful.

Older people may become overweight through insufficient exercise incorrect diet, or both. Obesity can be caused by certain medical conditions, and it is therefore advisable to have this possibility checked. Otherwise, simple exercise such as a short walk, if possible, may help, together with modifying the diet to include less fats and more unrefined carbohydrates. This will also help to prevent constipation. Advice can be obtained by the dietician concerning sufficient intake regarding vitamins, and so on.

Environmental Aspects

Older people living alone may be insensitive to temperature changes, or if they are not well off financially or forgetful, they may have difficulty in heating the house so that hypothermia is a possibility in some cases. Hypothermia may be defined as a condition arising when the body temperature falls to below 35 °C. If hypothermia is suspected, then obviously medical assistance should be requested. In the meantime, individuals should be covered lightly with a blanket, but no attempt should be made to warm them up suddenly; this needs to be done gradually. The only sure way of preventing hypothermia in people who may be at risk is to keep the room warm (around 20 °C is advised). Of heating fuels, gas is clearly easier to maintain than coal. Electricity and oil can be more expensive. Fires giving convected heat are more beneficial than those giving mainly radiant heat because the circulation of hot air is better. The various fuel companies will usually be able to advise about the best type of heater to have for the required use.

Heat also needs to be preserved, and this may be helped with several layers of clothing, double glazing, and sealing drafts from unused fireplaces or floorboards. Drafts are also more likely to occur if the rest of the house is cold, so it is desirable to have some warmth in other rooms. Heat loss may be reduced by having the attic insulated. Cavity-wall insulation can also be installed, although obviously consideration needs to be given to the length of time older people are likely to stay in the house; although such an improvement will normally add to the value of the house, it may take time to obtain the benefit through reduced heating bills.

Other types of insulation to consider include ensuring that cold water tanks and pipes in attics are well lagged to prevent freezing water and burst pipes in winter. Thick lagging on hot water tanks will help considerably to reduce heat loss. Immersion heaters can be fitted with time clocks so that they turn on and off automatically when required, and they also have a thermostat to adjust the temperature of the water.

Condensation can be a problem and results from the production of water vapor that then comes into contact with cold surfaces. The first step is to try to reduce the amount of water vapor. Gas, paraffin, and boiling water add water vapor to the air, so it is desirable not to use paraffin or bottled-gas appliances in houses in which condensation is already a problem. The second step is to try to keep the room warm and to ensure that there is some ventilation. In bathrooms and kitchens the problem can be reduced by using ceramic tiles on walls, although certain paints can be used that have a finish similar to gloss paint and that therefore help to prevent mold.

Emotional, Relationship, and Social Aspects

Your ability to care for elderly relatives will depend to some extent on the nature of the relationship that you have with them. If the relationship has always been difficult, then it is not likely to get any easier now. On the other hand, if the relationship has always been a relatively good one, then most difficulties will be overcome more easily. Older people do not tend to alter radically but tend to show previous personality traits in a more exaggerated form. Obviously, this is something of a generalization, but it is probably consistent with most people's experience. Exceptions to this include senile dementia, which causes a marked disintegration of the personality (this is discussed in a later chapter). In other cases, the experience of having to live with long-term disability may make elderly people depressed and feel wretched. However, whatever the nature of the relationship, caregivers need to detach themselves to the extent that they try to maintain a good degree of independence. It is also important that caregivers want to do it; otherwise there may be resentment and general difficulty in coping.

Sometimes caring for elderly people will mean popping in regularly to see how they are, but in other situations older people will actually move in with the caregiver and their family. Inevitably all members of the family will need to accept and adapt to this. Even though one person may be happy about it, other members of the family may not be. Obviously the arrangement will not work if there are strong views against it. The whole matter will usually require thorough discussion.

Elderly relatives themselves will take some time to adjust to the move, and there may be some initial problems to be sorted out. Where possible, elderly relatives should be given as much independence as possible. In some cases they may move into an adjoining "granny flat." In other cases they may move in with the family. They should be allowed to take part in domestic chores and take responsibilities within the family, just as other members do, within the limits of their capability. Some elderly people are happy to do very little; they are people who have probably always been a bit like that. Others may have been very active and independent, perhaps dominant, and they will need to feel useful around the house.

Part of maintaining independence involves things outside of the house. Elderly relatives should be encouraged to maintain existing social contacts and to continue in previous activities, interests, and hobbies as much as possible.

Physical independence should be treated similarly. Even though elderly people may be suffering disability caused by a stroke, for example, they should still be encouraged to dress and wash themselves, even though this may require additional aids and may take them very much longer. When assistance is required, this should be limited to the minimum necessary.

At all costs, elderly people should not be left sitting around unoccupied and with no demand placed on them. I return to this issue more than once in this book, but whatever the level of disability, almost all older people will react to some kind of stimulation, from a short walk in the fresh air or down to the shops to active participation in games, activities, and day-to-day events.

Elderly relatives should themselves recognize that the caregiver must retain some degree of independence. This means being able to go out of the house, to have friends, and to do things independently without feeling guilty and without arguments. This is part and parcel of any relationship, in fact, and caring for elderly relatives is no exception. There may, of course, be anxiety about leaving elderly relatives alone, but sometimes other family members or friends can pop in if it is not safe to leave them alone.

Getting in touch with the relevant volunteer and professional organizations early on will be advantageous because there are many services they can offer, and these will all help to ease the burden. The existence of these will vary from one area to another.

In many cases the caregiver will be a woman who is married and has children. She may also have a job. Each of these three things is a full-time occupation! Here there is likely to be stress because even the most energetic person will find it difficult to do all three things at the same time without one or other suffering. On the other hand, giving up the job may mean a reduction in the family income, which may be resented by other family members. It will also mean the loss of organized activity outside of the home that was previously an important source of personal fulfillment. The loss of a career may also be resented, for it may be difficult to return to it later. Work also offers a potential social life. All this needs to be considered, and in some cases it may be more workable to take on a full- or part-time caregiver.

In other instances the caregiver may be single. This is perhaps a less desirable situation. In the case of a married woman, other members of the family will still bring friends home and social life will be less disrupted; for a single person, social life may be more severely curtailed. This may be regretted later, especially perhaps if the chance for a lasting relationship with another person has been sacrificed.

The caregiver may be a woman looking after her husband and she herself is elderly. This may entail giving up her job, although more often she will be over the retirement age herself. Some role adaptation may be necessary, such as changing fuses (although in my experience fuses do not need changing very often!), dealing with financial affairs, and so on. However, the anxiety about such things is usually unnecessary, and such adaptation is not as difficult as many fear.

Of course, in many circumstances the caregiver will be a man looking after his wife. For him the problem may be one of doing domestic chores for the first time in his life! However, again, I have been struck by how well most men seem able to adapt to this role, and few seem to resent having to do domestic chores! Perhaps more difficult is the disappointment concerning retirement. Many men will have looked forward to these years, only to find that their hopes have been dashed.

Legal Aspects and Benefits

There are various legal provisions for dealing with elderly people who are failing mentally. There are also several benefits that are available in certain cases. Because these change from time to time, I do not discuss them in detail here. Rather, readers are advised to consult their lawyer and social worker to inquire about allowances.

REFERENCES AND FURTHER READING

Agate, J. (1979). *Taking care of old people at home.* London: Unwin.

Dartington, T. (1980). *Family care of old people.* London: Souvenir.

Pattie, A., & Gilleard, C. (1979). *The Clifton Assessment Procedures for the Elderly.* Sevenoaks, Kent, England: Hodder & Stoughton.

3

Anxiety and Depression

ANXIETY

Let me begin by putting anxiety into perspective. A certain degree of anxiety is normal and indeed is essential for our well-being. Everybody has experienced, and from time to time does experience, some anxiety. This anxiety may be about something very tangible and temporary, such as the experience of stage fright, or it may be about something more complicated such as a relationship problem. It may vary in degree so that on the one hand, although we may feel anxious, we can nevertheless force ourselves to face the feared situation; on the other hand, however, the fear may be so intense that we tend to avoid the situation. Thus, some degree of anxiety is normal, and as a rough rule of thumb we might conclude that anxiety is only abnormal when it begins to interfere with our daily lives, when it makes us ill, or leads us to resort to drugs or when it incapacitates and restricts us to the extent that our psychological health and social life may be at risk. First, I examine what I mean by the terms *anxiety, fear, tension,* and *stress.*

Anxiety and *fear* tend to refer to relatively temporary situations, temporary in the sense that we experience the fear or anxiety for as long as we are thinking about or experiencing the threatening situation. When the threatening event has passed, the anxiety tends to dissipate, even though it may return the next time the event or thought occurs. Strictly speaking, fear refers more to the feeling we have in a specific situation, whereas anxiety might be used more correctly to describe a feeling we might have in a more general situation. Here, however, I use the word *anxiety* to refer to a particular set of symptoms that tend to be experienced in a threatening situation. I use the word *tension* to describe one such particular symptom, which is muscular tension or tightness. *Stress,* on the other hand, can be thought of more as a long-standing problem, because, unlike anxiety, it does not come and go quickly. People may be said to be under stress when the demands made by the environment, including any demands that people make on themselves, exceed the capabilities of the individuals for meeting the demands. Anxiety may therefore be present when people are experiencing stress, but it should now be clear that the two are not interchangeable and that anxiety refers more to a symptom or set of symptoms that may be a part of stress or may exist as a reaction to a more circumscribed situation.

Most people have fears of some sort that are usually minor in the sense that they can easily be avoided or coped with. People might have a fear of snakes, but because snakes need never be encountered in their daily lives, this is unlikely to be a problem. A fear of dogs, on the other hand, could be more problematic because there is a much greater likelihood of encountering one. Anxiety symptoms may be experienced at both physical and psychological levels. The heart tends to beat more rapidly, the rate of breathing may increase, there may be "butterflies" in the stomach, dry mouth, tightness of the mouth and throat, and nausea. There may be a feeling of faintness, light-headedness, or dizziness, there may also be tingling or numbness in the fingers. People may have a strong desire to escape from the situation or to hide. Oddly enough, some people may actively seek situations that are potentially anxiety provoking. Such situations range from watching horror films to racing in cars or performing stunt tricks. A certain degree of anxiety is not bad for us, and indeed it has been shown that performance improves with some degree of anxiety but that it declines beyond a certain level. Too little anxiety might lead to carelessness and a greater tendency to make mistakes, whereas too much anxiety might cause us to rush or make more mistakes.

Another feature of anxiety is that it may not be experienced immediately. People who have a near-miss while driving their car may not experience the anxiety until some moments later when the crisis has well passed. This delay between event and anxiety may be as long as several hours.

Stress may be caused by both external and internal factors. External events by themselves can be stress producing even in people who would consider themselves to be normal and level-headed, events such as difficulties with their job and relationship difficulties at home or at work. Internal events can also be stressful, such as setting unrealistic standards of performance to achieve. Clearly, internal and external events can occur together to produce stress. It is somewhat likely that some degree of stress can be avoided altogether, but at mild levels the mind and body can develop and utilize methods of adapting or coping analogous to the body developing and bringing into action defenses against bodily infection. When stress is more severe, such coping methods may be overstretched and as a result, symptoms may be experienced or people may begin to behave in an uncharacteristic or maladaptive way.

Short-term stress is little different from the kind of anxiety that I have just described. Our mind and body are able to produce a reaction that potentially helps us. If suddenly threatened by seeing a car rapidly approaching while crossing the road, anxiety helps us by allowing us to respond very quickly and (hopefully!) avoid being run over. If attacked by another person, either verbally or physically, anxiety allows us to respond appropriately. When the threatening event has passed we return to normal.

Problems occur, however, when stress is prolonged and there is a long-term demand on our resources to combat it.

The analogy would be a long-term illness that uses up considerable amounts of the body's defenses, leaving people weak and vulnerable.

The physiological response in short-term stress situations is not usually problematic. Our resources are called on, but only temporarily; these can be replenished before a second threatening event occurs. However, in long-term stress the defense systems are in constant use, demand may exceed supply, and there is no period when replenishment can take place. In very severe circumstances, the system ceases to be able to cope and we may suffer a nervous breakdown. When long-term stress is present there may be warning signs. A long-term increase in heart rate may result in an increased probability of heart malfunction. There may be a tendency not to take care of ourselves very well, pushing ourselves to the limit despite the feeling of a need to rest, or not taking the time necessary to get over an illness. So much for physical factors. Let me now consider emotional or psychological factors.

Anxiety and depression are part and parcel of stress. Both anxiety and depression may lead to sleeping and eating problems, loss of interest, irritability, and poor concentration. Anxiety may produce physiological symptoms of the kind just described, guilt, and general feelings of apprehension. Muscular tension may lead to aches and pains and tiredness. We may become preoccupied with ourselves and worry about developing illnesses. Depression leads to feelings of hopelessness, worthlessness, loss of self-esteem, and pessimism. We may be led to utilize maladaptive behaviors to blot symptoms out: excessive smoking or drinking, staying in bed, or in the extreme, attempting suicide.

Long-term stress may lead people to take it out on others. The family is often the first to suffer because feelings are more likely to be freely expressed at home. However, friends and work colleagues may also be subjected to unreasonable behavior. In either case, relationships may suffer, sometimes to the point where the damage is hard to repair. The problem then becomes circular because relationship problems and failures are additional causes of stress. People may demand more sympathy from others and feel sorry for themselves. They may feel that they no longer enjoy living but that they just exist.

Let me now look at anxiety in older people. Anxiety, as defined by clinical criteria, has been estimated to occur in some 7% of men and 17% of women in their later years. In elderly people anxiety often occurs with depression, hypochondriasis, or both; this being so, the treatment and management is as follows for these conditions: Occasionally, the anxiety may be quite specific in nature, so that elderly people develop a phobia or obsession about a particular situation, but often these are related to depression. A common type of this anxiety in older people is a fear of falling, going out of the house, crossing roads, and so forth. As a result of their fear, they then become housebound and depressed. The original anxiety may have had a realistic basis, such as physical weakness, the possibility of slipping on icy pavements, or of losing balance.

There are many other possible causes of anxiety in elderly people, many of them with a realistic basis. These are just a few examples. There may be financial difficulties or worries about whether they can maintain their independence and for how long. Older people may be afraid to go out for fear of being mugged. They may be afraid to go to certain places or to meet certain people because of possible embarrassment due, for example, to a fear of being incontinent or of falling.

In some cases anxiety may be associated with the *hyperventilation syndrome*. Hyperventilation simply means overbreathing. Some people, when confronted by a situation that is anxiety provoking, respond by starting to breathe rapidly and deeply. Now, this would be useful if they are running a race, but if they are standing or sitting still, carbon dioxide concentrations are reduced in the blood stream because the carbon dioxide is being eliminated more rapidly. Now, when carbon dioxide is in solution in water, it produces acidity (carbonic acid) so that when its concentration is reduced, the blood stream will become less acid. This condition is called *respiratory alkalosis*. Even relatively limited amounts of hyperventilation can cause a condition called *alkalosis*. The reduction of acidity in the body tissues leads to a whole range of altered functions, including some affecting the nervous system. This has the effect of further increasing the anxiety level so that people feel an impending sense of catastrophy, that they are going to die or lose control. Not uncommonly, patients complain of dizziness or light-headedness, palpitations, headaches, trembling, and anxiety. Getting hyperventilating people to breathe in and out of a paper bag for a minute or two is often effective treatment because the carbon dioxide levels in the bloodstream are soon rectified this way.

Anxiety may sometimes be associated with a particular situation or event, such as a fear of snakes, spiders, dogs, or whatever, in which case the condition is usually called a *phobia*. Many people do not like spiders, but this is not the same as having a phobia. A patient with a phobia of, say, dogs is quite incapacitiated and unable to go out of the house alone for fear of meeting one.

Anxiety may also be associated with a compulsion to carry out a certain act. Some people, when they become anxious, may respond by feeling the compulsion to repeatedly carry out some unnecessary activity, such as counting up to a hundred or washing their hands repeatedly. Such conditions are called *obsessive–compulsive neuroses*.

In elderly people, obsessive–compulsive problems do not appear to be very common, and indeed neither do phobias. As noted earlier, their anxieties seem more often to be associated with practical problems, such as how they are going to cope on a low income or how they are going to manage to keep up their housework. In other cases they will have specific fears, such as a fear of falling, but strictly speaking it would seem inaccurate to call this a phobia in the true sense because their fear may have quite a realistic basis. For example, people who have suffered a stroke may be afraid of falling during physiotherapy sessions in which they are being taught to walk again.

The first stage in management is to try to isolate the cause of the anxiety. Sometimes this will be easy, such as the example of fear of falling. On other occasions the fear may be less focal and may relate to a general anxiety about aging and death. Anxiety should be considered seriously. It will not be helpful to tell elderly people to pull themselves together or to stop worrying. It may be necessary to spend time discussing what the various fears are making it clear that you are sympathetic and understand the problem.

The next stage is to devise a simple program for dealing with the anxiety. Take the example of fear of falling. Obviously, one needs to assess any weakness elderly people have and to ensure that any required aid is available. However, once their level of capability has been established, they should be encouraged to overcome their anxiety through a procedure called *desensitization.* In practice, this means setting a short distance at first for them to walk, perhaps with some assistance as necessary. When they can achieve this, it is then appropriate to move to the next target, which will be walking a little bit farther with a little less assistance. Approaching the problem in this way will help them to overcome the anxiety in easily manageable amounts, whereas the thought of immediately walking all the way down to the shops may be so anxiety provoking as to ensure that they avoid walking altogether.

Most specific anxieties can be managed in this way, but more general fears may need a different approach. Financial worries, for example, may be quite realistic; it may help to sit down and go through everything in fine detail with elderly people with the aim of working out a suitable budget. There may be better ways of organizing the payment of bills. Quarterly and half-yearly bills can often be paid monthly. This is useful because the total annual amount can be divided into 12 equal amounts. The higher bills in winter, which are a major source of financial worry for many elderly people, can thus be avoided.

Fears of burglary or mugging may need practical measures to assist with reducing anxiety, such as fitting bolts to the doors, installing some kind of intruder alarm, or other similar device. When anxious thoughts persist, it is appropriate to try to teach elderly people some of the techniques for dealing with inappropriate thoughts (I consider this in a moment). Finally, getting them to do some form of relaxation exercises and looking at other stress control measures may be appropriate (see chapter 7).

Anxiety may occur within the context of confusion in elderly people. For example, people who are disoriented in time and place will have difficulty recognizing and making sense of their environment. This can be a frightening experience. Similarly, people who cannot remember things from one moment to the next may fear that they have lost control of themselves and may seek constant help from others. In both of these cases, it is important to understand the cause of the anxiety and to take the approach for dealing with memory-disordered and disoriented elderly people that is described in chapter 4.

Anxiety may result from physical problems or impairments. For example patients who have suffered a stroke may fear having another one. Residual symptoms such as speech deficits may lead to anxiety. A period of time spent in hospital may lead them to worry about how things are going at home; at discharge there may be a period of time during which they have difficulty readjusting. In these cases, as in the other examples given, there is a tangible, understandable, and rational basis to the anxiety. It is not so much that elderly people have things out of perspective, neither is it necessarily the case that their anxiety stems from basic feelings of inadequacy or dependency as may happen in younger persons. Rather, elderly people may be facing genuine difficulties for the first time of their life. They may fear being unable to manage day-to-day life demands. The treatment of anxiety in elderly people, therefore, may not always be the same as in younger people. There may be more practical considerations as well as a need for individual counseling and support at a psychological level.

DEPRESSION

To the layperson, the term *depression* probably means feeling down in the dumps and wretched. Although this is a characteristic feature of depression, it is in fact only one of many different but related symptoms that make up the clinical condition. Second, the clinical condition refers to depression as a state prevailing over a period of time, not just the odd day here or there.

Depression is somewhat difficult to define, but there are certain general features that do occur and that I discuss later. These features include physical, psychological, and social aspects. Although elderly people are no more likely to become depressed than younger people, there seems little doubt that depression accounts for many referrals to mental health professionals who work with elderly people.

Depression tends to reach a peak in the middle years, and at that time of life it is more often mild. In later years the depression is more frequently severe; in such cases, suicide is more likely to occur.

Perhaps because of differences in defining depression, research studies have varied widely in their estimates of the size of the problem, but it seems probable that clinical depression may affect 3–4% of older men and perhaps 6% of older women. The reason for this sex difference is not clear.

I use the term *clinical depression* to underscore the fact that surveys of this kind do not necessarily include what laypeople may consider to be depression. Everyone, from time to time, has periods of feeling low, hopeless, and so on, but these would not be considered to reach clinical severity. Clinical depression would be said to occur if symptoms are severe enough that they interfere with everyday functioning and if they are relatively prolonged.

In elderly people depression often leads to an impairment in functions such as memory and speed of responding, so that depressed elderly people may appear to be confused or demented (I look at these terms in more detail in chapter 4). Any such impairment often, but not always, improves as the depression lifts. However, there is considerable individual variation that makes it difficult to provide an accurate general description.

Some people become withdrawn, apathetic, unresponsive, and slow. Others become agitated, restless, and demanding. Generally, though, certain features occur with regularity and are as follows: (a) alteration in mood (sadness, possibly agitation, possibly varying throughout the day); (b) negative self-concept (the person thinks little of himself or herself, and this may reach the extent of feelings of sinfulness, guilt, and hallucinations); (c) self-punitive thought and behavior; (d) slowness; (e) loss of sleep, reduction in sex drive, and loss of appetite; and (f) reductions in intellectual and memory capacities. In older people one often sees a preoccupation with the body and its functions, so that they may feel excessively worried about the function of their bowels or feel that their insides are rotting.

There is also general agreement that depression takes one of two main forms. The first kind is relatively mild; in these cases the mood is less severely affected, there is day-to-day variation, and there are no false beliefs or hallucinations. The depression may or may not be occurring for the first time, but it will usually be related to various life events experienced by the individual.

The second kind is characterized by a more severe mood disorder; feelings of guilt; and loss of appetite, sex drive, and sleep, with a variation through the day and possibly with the occurrence of false beliefs and hallucinations. This type of depression may be related to chemical changes more than to life events. Some still argue that these two types are part of a single continuum, but this is a minority view. In some cases depression is part of a disorder called manic, or bipolar, depression, in which severe depressive episodes can alternate with bouts of extreme elation of mood and hyperactivity. However, these disorders tend to start earlier in life; I do not discuss them in further detail here because they are not specific to elderly people.

However, hypochondriacal behavior is often related to depression, so I do mention it here. Hypochondriacal people become convinced that they have at least one, although as often as not, many physical disorders. They may complain of a wide range of discomforts, ailments, aches, and pains. As I have noted, elderly people are quite likely to suffer from some degree of aches and pains at some time, but most are able to learn to cope with them. Hypochondriacal patients, on the other hand, tend to complain repeatedly about their discomforts and may continually visit their doctor with a new or persisting symptom, believing that something is seriously wrong. This can make them unpopular patients and earns them the reputation of being a nuisance. They tend to gain little sympathy from even the most patient people. Relatives may be telephoned frequently, perhaps at inconvenient times, and relationships may suffer as a result. The complaint sometimes takes the form of a life-threatening disease such as cancer. The picture is complicated by the possibility of a factual basis to elderly people's worries. In other cases pain may arise due to tension, which in turn results from strain in relationships. I recall one elderly lady who was referred for treatment for tension headaches that were long-standing, persistent, and had not responded to medical treatment. On meeting the patient's husband, it became clear the there was a great deal of strain in the marital relationship, but both denied this. However, the patient's headaches always improved when she was away from her husband.

In other instances in which, for example, elderly people live alone, social isolation and lack of sensory input mean that they may become increasingly absorbed in their pain. Complaining of it may bring a response from others. Many elderly people have difficulty seeing their problems at a psychological level and express their emotional difficulties in terms of physical problems such as constipation, pain, and malaise. Therefore, pain and "illness behavior" should not always be seen literally; it may be their way of saying that they need emotional help. Whether they themselves can see this is, however, another matter!

WHAT CAUSES DEPRESSION?

I have already noted in passing that some types of depression may be caused by chemical changes, whereas others seem to be explained by psychological and social factors.

A detailed discussion of the former is beyond the scope of this book, but a number of psychological explanations have been proposed that I now briefly consider.

There are various theories of depression, the simplest of which is a *behavioral model*. This theory proposes that depression occurs when a person's behavior is no longer reinforced. *Reinforcement* here refers to a process by which behavior is encouraged. If people do something that leads to a pleasant outcome, then that behavior is said to have been rewarded. The behavior is thus strengthened, and there is an increase in the probability of the same behavior occurring again. (I discuss more about behavioral theories in chapter 5). This theory has been a relatively popular one for explaining depression in elderly people. A reduction in physical mobility, for example, would mean that many activities may be curtailed, more effort may be needed to achieve a particular goal, and some degree of discomfort or pain may be experienced in the process. The motivation to perform the task may therefore decline. General life changes such as retirement may lead to a reduced interaction with others and less of an opportunity for behavior to be reinforced. Earlier on in life people may have been encouraged by the rewards and praises of others, and social interaction in itself will have been an important source of well-being. However, this theory fails to account adequately for depression in elderly people. Clearly, many elderly people experience losses, reduction in activity, and so on, but only a minority become depressed.

Another theory of depression is called *learned helplessness*. This theory proposes that a state is reached whereby people can see no way out of their predicament or fail to maintain a feeling of control. This may lead them to giving up doing things that they can still do and that would otherwise help them. This theory has some tangible basis to the extent that many of the negative changes occurring in elderly people's life are ones that do not readily lead to a feeling of being able to do something about them. Such changes include the death of one's partner or permanent and progressive disability. As I show later in this book, depression is

a normal phase in the bereavement process. It is easy to en-
visage how people who have suffered such losses may have
difficulty in mantaining a sense of being able to control their
life.

There is some evidence that this theory has some basis
for explaining depression in elderly people because it has
been found that they are less likely to feel depressed if they
have a greater sense of control over their lives. This theory
is an improvement on the behavioral theory because it refers
to some extent to the meaning of loss and therefore allows
for the fact that the effects of changes in old age vary in
their impact from person to person.

An alternative and possibly more popular theory places
more emphasis on depressive thoughts. Depressed people
are seen to present three main features: a negative view of
themselves (seeing themselves as inadequate); a negative
view of the world (everyday experiences are seen nega-
tively); and a negative view of the future (an expectation
that current difficulties will continue). The central feature
of this theory is that it proposes that people feel depressed
because they are thinking in a depressive way. This leads to
the prediction that if depressed thinking can be prevented or
altered, then they will feel better. Typically, depressed people see events in a negative way. Thus, even if they have
achieved something with a degree of success, they will tend
to greatly underestimate the achievement or perhaps even
see themselves as having failed. This model of depression
fits in very well with what I have already said about the
difficulty some older people seem to have in accepting that
they need to make targets easier and to accept a lowering of
standards in their level of functioning. If the target is beyond reach, elderly people will easily find themselves thinking that they should have done better. A second tendency is
to see only the negative aspects of a situation and fail to see
the positive aspects. A third common occurrence is to misinterpret an event, and more especially to blame oneself for
the outcome. An example of this would be people who pass a
friend in the street, but the friend fails to acknowledge
them. People who think depressively will attribute this fail-

ure to themselves, perhaps by thinking that they have said or done something to upset the other person, whereas a more probable reason is that the other person simply did not see them.

That theory of depression would seem to account reasonably well for this disorder in elderly people, although it would still probably be necessary to suppose that there is a degree of individual susceptibility to becoming depressed because, as I have already said, the majority of older people do not become depressed despite many negative events in their life, and of those who do it is often for the first time.

Work by researchers such as Brown and Harris (1978) has also shed light on the environmental factors associated with depression. They found that depression tended to be associated with various "life events" such as loss of job, relocation, disappointment or financial loss, serious illness, and separation or death of other. They also found that certain conditions made for greater vulnerability to the effects of such life events. These included the lack of a person in whom to confide, lack of employment, three or more young children at home, and separation from one's mother before the age of 11. Of course, this research was conducted with younger people, but it is clear from research by Murphy (1982) that in elderly people, the effect of life events can be even more serious, with depression being associated with major life problems, physical infirmity, and social problems. She found that working-class elderly people were more likely to become depressed and that this was related to poorer health and to social problems. Lack of a confiding relationship was found to increase vulnerability to depression, and this was reported to be a life-long pattern of behavior.

Having looked briefly at some theories of depression, I now look at what can be done to alleviate it.

TREATMENT OF DEPRESSION

First of all, depression often gets better without specific help. However, when it does not or if it is more severe or

persists, then professional treatment is indicated. It is difficult to be precise about the response to treatment shown by
depressed people. Severity need not be an indicator because
even very severely depressed people can make remarkable
recoveries, whereas milder cases can persist. The outcome
probably depends more on the cause of the depression, the
extent of negative life events, the meaning of these for the
individual, and whether positive changes can be made. On
the average, it is probably not too inaccurate to say that
about two-thirds of depressed people either recover or stay
the same, although it must be said that older people seem
less able to recover than younger ones. Also, depression in
elderly people often tends to recur.

It is obviously beyond the scope of this book to deal in
great detail with medical and psychological treatments of depression; rather, the aim here is to inform the caregiver of
the main treatment methods.

If elderly people do become depressed to the extent that
their behavior is affected and their ability to function is reduced, then the first stage is to visit your physician, or better to ask for a home visit, because it is often far more helpful to assess elderly people in their own home than in the
hospital. Seeing older people at home will give many clues as
to their present level of functioning and the extent to which
they are coping. You may ask for a visit from a psychiatrist
who specializes in the care of elderly people and who may
have a team of other professionals working with him or her.
It may be thought helpful to prescribe medical treatments,
which in the case of depression will include either antide-
pressant medication or electroconvulsive therapy (ECT) or
both. Many readers may be unfamiliar with the term *ECT*, so
I explain this briefly.

Many people do fear ECT, and there is no doubt that the
public have been provided with much negative information
about this method of treatment. Within the professions of
psychiatry and psychology, there has been much debate over
the years about the therapeutic use of ECT. The fear concerning ECT probably has to do with the idea of electrical
current being passed, but the procedure is quite safe and

painless; the patients have no experience of it because they are unconscious while it is administered. There has been some dispute concerning whether ECT produces memory loss; although there is usually some degree of amnesia immediately after the treatment, there is no evidence that lasting memory impairment occurs. Many people have been helped by ECT, and for elderly people it is often more effective and safer than antidepressive medication.

There are different types of antidepressive medication, some of which may be taken only if certain things are not drunk or eaten, but you will be advised if this is the case. Antidepressive drugs often take several weeks to start to work, so immediate effects should not be expected. Also, there may be side effects such as dry mouth. You may be warned about this beforehand, but if side effects do persist and are troublesome, then it is perfectly alright to mention this to the doctor. He or she may advise you that the medication be continued despite the side effects or may prescribe an alternative.

In other cases, or in combination with antidepressants, psychotherapy may be offered. This is sometimes carried out by a clinical psychologist or other member of the team with a relevant qualification. Psychotherapy focuses on attempting to discover the psychological factors relevant to the person's depression, defining these in terms that are understandable and amenable to change and then devising methods to do so.

In a previous chapter I discussed some of the general things that older people can consider doing in order to make a better adjustment to the aging process. However, even when people do become depressed, many of these should be considered helpful in getting them better. It unfortunately still happens that people who become depressed are told to pull themselves together, cheer up, think positively, and other unhelpful things. If they could do this for themselves, then they would surely do so! What they do require is someone to show them what they can do in order to feel better. Professional help, when available and when required, is aimed at this, but there is much that can be done by taking the right approach.

It is likely that those who have had high expectations of themselves and others in the past may have more difficulty in accepting disability now. Others who may be more vulnerable are those who have put, as it were, all their eggs in one basket. People who only had one interest and who can no longer do this because of some disability have little to fall back on. Highly obsessional and perfectionistic people may also be more prone to depression, again because they find it hard to accept a change in their level of ability.

In any work of this kind, it is important for the person who is trying to help to have three main qualities. These are empathy, warmth, and genuineness, qualities that have been stressed by the psychologist Carl Rogers (1951). People who are emotionally troubled will be helped by the person who is empathic and shows signs of understanding concern, by the person who listens carefully, is relaxed, and who puts across a feeling of genuine interest. The helping person needs to be patient, tolerant, and have insight into suffering. If the person does not possess or cannot develop these characteristics, it is less likely that he or she will be able to help. However, there are certain potential difficulties in helping and caring for others. It is important to be able to develop some kind of limit in terms of emotional involvement. It is not infrequent for volunteer workers, and indeed sometimes even professionally trained people, to themselves become overinvolved emotionally. This can lead to emotional exhaustion: No one is built to withstand continual levels of stress, and working with others who are emotionally troubled is, of course, stressful.

Setting limits usually comes with experience, but it is important to keep in mind. It is necessary to ensure that while you are trying to help other people, you can only do this if you agree to the terms of the helping relationship; this is not always very easy with relatives who are used to a different kind of relationship. They now have to accept the role of the "patient" who accepts help from you. Setting limits means sticking to strict terms and on occasions asserting yourself without feeling guilty. Professional staff can often prevent problems in this area by working in teams. Discussions about patients are made by the group, and the individual is never left with the feeling that he or she alone is responsible for the care of the patient. Mutual support between caregivers is therefore very important.

How do you help depressed people? First, you have to ensure that quick and meaningful rewards can be given when required. Praise and immediate feedback for a correct response is often enough. However, make sure that your praise sounds genuine and that you really are pleased with their response; otherwise it will appear false and will be ineffective. In practice this means setting a target that is attainable and immediately rewarding success in achieving it. If they fail to reach the target, keep simplifying it until some response is obtained. As targets are reached, gradually increase them.

Second, it is useful to try to steer them away from thinking about their disability and to get them to try to concentrate on their residual skills. Encourage them to continue with previous interests and to restart old hobbies and activities that are still within their grasp.

Third, it is important to remember that feelings of depression may come from depressive thoughts, as described above in accordance with the theory proposed by the psychologist Aaron Beck (1976). Depressed people tend to have a negative self-image and to interpret events in a negative way. Therefore, it is important to try to change the negative thinking in people who are depressed. Try to get them to realize the sequence of external events and their reactions to them, as in the above minor example of passing a friend in the street who fails to notice them, and get them to put this into practice when producing negative interpretations to events. Teach them that an interpretation is just that: It is not "I know" or "That is a fact," but "I think something or other happened." Again, with the example of the friend in the street, demonstrate that the event could be interpreted in many different ways and that attributing the event to oneself is only one interpretation. Stereotyped themes should be highlighted so that themes emerging from automatic thoughts are challenged: Challenge thoughts concerned with poverty, inferiority, loss, and so on. They may need to be taught that certain feelings and thoughts are not bad but healthy and necessary. They may, for example, believe that they should never become angry: Show examples of when anger is appropriate and how it makes them feel better to express themselves. Every time they produce a negative utterance, this should be challenged, and every time they have a depressive thought you should teach them to challenge it themselves and entertain alternative thoughts. Sometimes, of course, the negative thought will be factual and irrefutable. In these cases try to get them to prevent such negative thoughts and to think of something more positive. They can be taught to prevent such thoughts by saying "stop" to themselves every time an unwanted or negative thought comes to mind. They should then concentrate on trying to develop a more positive thought or action. Thought stopping is actually quite a difficult procedure with which to achieve a result. After a while the negative thought will return, so the procedure should be used repetitively.

So much for depressive thoughts, but there are other important things to do. You may have noticed that, especially when you feel that you have achieved little at work or elsewhere, that the successful completion of a tangible, even if simple, everyday activity at home leads to a feeling of accomplishment. Depressed people will feel this lack of achievement, and it is therefore important to try to get them to carry out such tasks, no matter how trivial or routine the tasks may seem; this will help to counter their view that they can do nothing. It is important, too, to do some exercise rather than sit still doing nothing. Try to get them involved in some sort of task to keep them occupied and busy, preferably something that has a reasonably rapid result. Activity in itself, of course, will not cure the depression, but it is one part of the overall treatment approach. Unpleasant events should be avoided as much as possible, and elderly people should be exposed to as many pleasant ones as possible. This may seem obvious, but it is worth making a list of things that they do and do not find pleasant as a basis to go on.

Particularly problematic are hypochondriacal people. There is always the danger that even though it always turns out there is nothing seriously amiss, they may cry wolf once too often and eventually have a serious illness. This always makes it difficult to avoid treating them as having a potential illness on every occasion. Such behavior will often have persisted for years and is so overlearned, its origins so obscure, and its role in their repertoire so central that effective treatment is very hard. Theoretically, an approach based on not reinforcing their utterances about their physical state should eventually bring about a reduction in the amount of time they spend doing this. This may be done by setting limits in terms of the length of time they may talk about their pain or disorder. Outside of these limits, the behavior would then be ignored or they would be reminded that they are talking too much about their symptoms and at the wrong time. However, attempts to confront the behavior directly by responses such as "You are exaggerating" or "You must be imagining it" are not likely to be helpful and should be avoided. Their experiences should not be denied. Care should be taken to try to maintain an empathic, warm, and caring relationship; at the same time, ensure that you are firm and assertive about the degree of behavior acceptable. It should be agreed that additional reward or attention can be available only after an acceptable period of time has elapsed without "pain talk." They should also be encouraged, rewarded, and praised for engaging in meaningful and appropriate activity and conversation. Such an approach needs to be applied consistently and by all those who are likely to interact with them. Initially there may be an increase in pain talk, but theoretically this should eventually decrease.

If they are taking medication for pain, then this should be taken at set intervals rather than as required; however, this should be worked out with the physician if the medication is by prescription. Subjective complaints about pain may be worse if they are anxious, and some of the methods discussed in a later chapter on stress and stress management may be appropriately applied.

REFERENCES AND FURTHER READING

Beck, A. (1976). *Cognitive therapy and the emotional disorders.* New York: International University Press.

Brown, G. W., & Harris, T. (1978). *Social origins of depression.* London: Tavistock.

Marks, I. M. (1978). *Living with fear.* London: McGraw-Hill.

Murphy, E. (1982). Social origins of depression in old age. *British Journal of Psychiatry, 141,* 135–142.

Rogers, C. (1951). *Client-centred therapy.* London: Constable.

4

Dementia

Dementia is a collective term that refers to a number of psychological disorders occurring predominantly, although not exclusively, in old age that are characterized by progressive mental deterioration due to degeneration of the central nervous system.

There are several basic misunderstandings about dementia that need to be corrected. The first misunderstanding that can occur is that all elderly people suffer from dementia, whereas, as I show in a moment, it affects only a relatively small number. Second, it is not a disorder that is exclusive to elderly people. There are cases of dementia in middle age or even earlier. It does, however, become more common with increasing age.

For many years little advance was made in our understanding of dementia, but it is now commonly referred to as the disease of the century. There are several reasons for recent interest in the disorder. First of all, it is clear that dementia is a pressing public health problem and has become so largely because of the advancing life expectancy and the resulting increase of the proportion of older people in the population. Interest in dementia has also been prompted by research into its causes. Advanced technology has increased our knowledge about chemicals in the brain known as *neurotrasmitters*. At the moment it is unclear to what extent the causes of dementia relate to neurotransmitter disturbances, but investigations in this direction have led to attempts to remedy the disease through chemical therapy. Developments have also occurred in investigatory techniques so that we now have better methods of examining the brain and can actually see changes within it.

I could discuss various definitions of dementia, but this is not very useful because, as will become clear later, so many different deficits occur that it becomes difficult to find a definition to cover all of the eventualities. More useful is to give a description of the more common forms of the disease. However, generally speaking, one can think of dementia as a progressive loss of intellect arising from the deterioration in the nerve cells in the brain and resulting in an impairment in everyday functioning. This is a somewhat loose description, but what I am referring to is basically a loss of intellectual function quite in excess of that expected by the normal aging process. Dementia also refers to an acquired loss of intellectual function as opposed to mental retardation in which the intellect was never properly acquired in the first place. There are many types of dementia and many causes. Some result from, for example, anoxia (lack of oxygen to the brain) or cerebrovascular accidents (strokes). Other forms of dementia can be caused by toxic substances such as long-term alcohol or barbiturate abuse.

PREVALENCE

What is the size of the problem? Below the age of 65 the prevalence appears to be very small. Between the ages of 45 and 54, it has been estimated that about 0.025% of the population is affected, rising to around 0.072% up to the age of 64. From 65 to 69 the prevalence is 2.1%, increasing only slightly to 3.3% for the 70–74 age group. In the 75–79 age range, the prevalence rises again to 8%, and it has been estimated that some 18% of those over 80 suffer from the disease. Quite clearly, then, there is an increasing risk of developing dementia as one becomes older, but it should be noted that even in those over 80 a large number of people remain relatively unaffected.

TYPES OF DEMENTIA

Dementias may be classified in a number of ways, for example, by age of onset, cause, underlying pathology, or response to treatment. However, diagnostically it is quite common to classify dementias according to the areas of the brain affected. There are, of course, drawbacks to this, but it is generally agreed that this provides the most rational basis for the purposes of diagnosis. However, for purposes of discussion I consider some of the more common forms of dementia without going into great detail about which parts of the brain are affected most.

Alzheimer's disease is the first port of call. This term is used to refer to certain cases of dementia that occur under the age of 65. However, it is now considered that this is purely arbitrary and that the most common form of dementia in older people is in fact Alzheimer's disease, accounting for perhaps as many as three-quarters of all dementia cases. Alzheimer's disease, then, may begin in middle age or earlier but increases in prevelance with age. When dementia is being referred to in old age, therefore, it is most commonly Alzheimer's disease; for this reason I refer to this disease in most of this chapter. It is characterized by intellectual and memory loss, but there may also be emotional and personality changes, together with more specific losses in comprehension, speech, perception, and action. The condition progresses, usually gradually rather than suddenly, with these signs becoming more apparent in the process, until patients become incontinent and require constant nursing care.

Another example of dementia, although one that is less common, is Pick's disease. The clinical presentation is not dissimilar to Alzheimer's disease, thus making the differential diagnosis a difficult one. However, speech abnormalities are frequent and memory impairment tends to be less marked. Pick's disease is associated with damage to the front of the brain, an area referred too appropriately as the *frontal lobes*. It is this part of the brain that has often been associated with, among other things, personality. This is in contrast to Alzheimer's disease in which damage to the temporal lobes, farther back in the brain, occurs. The temporal lobes are known to play an important part in memory, and if they are damaged memory loss will often ensue.

There are other dementias in which the brain damage is also relatively localized. One example is multi-infarct dementia, which happens to be the second most common type of dementia in elderly people. An *infarct* refers to a type of stroke that occurs in a blood vessel, and so this form of dementia progresses by means of repeated strokes. With each stroke there may be noticeable decline, and the progression of multi-infarct dementia tends therefore to be stepwise, in contrast to the more insidious deterioration seen in Alzheimer's disease. However, the picture is complicated somewhat by the fact that some elderly people suffer from both Alzheimer's and multi-infarct dementia. Multi-infarct dementia is characterized by many of the features of Alzheimer's disease, but personality changes are usually marked, and patients are often described as being depressed, irritable, and apathetic.

There are many other types of dementia. These are less common, and in the majority of cases, as I have shown, elderly people will be suffering from Alzheimer's disease. Therefore, in the remainder of this chapter, I refer primarily to this disorder.

ALZHEIMER'S DISEASE

The disease is so called because of its first description by a neurologist named Alois Alzheimer in 1907. He described the case of a 51-year-old woman who began to show memory lapses but who went on to develop a severe dementia. At postmortem it was found that her brain had shrunk in size and had undergone a number of abnormal changes.

The exact presentation will obviously vary from case to case and will depend to some extent on factors such as the areas of the brain affected and patients' previous personality. There are, however, certain general features. These are well described by Miller (1977). The first of these is intellectual impairment. This will present itself in the form of patients having difficulty with tasks that they once found easy. There will be difficulty in learning new information and a disturbance of thought processes, particularly abstract reasoning. On psychological tests of intelligence, it is usually found that although they may retain a good vocabulary, be able to read words, and display a reasonable general knowledge, their reasoning powers, ability to perform arithmetic calculations, and comprehension of events may be impaired. They usually present difficulties in solving novel problems, often having problems in orienting things correctly, and their actions may be noticeably slower. Simple constructional abilities such as drawing a house in perspective may prove difficult.

Memory loss is a central and usually very evident feature. In fact, it will often be the first to be noticed by a relative. Of course, many older people complain of poor memory, but on closer examination it often turns out that they perform quite well on memory tests. The memory impairment in Alzheimer's disease, however, is detectable on psychological tests. They may have difficulty in recalling recent events and learning new information. This may become so severe that information may be lost in a matter of minutes. Sooner or later disorientation occurs and they fail to remember the day of the week or the year. They may become lost in places that are familiar to them and fail to realize where they are. Missing information in memory may be filled by confabulation, so that they may provide a quite fictitious and highly improbable account of what has recently happened. They may appear to regress in age and may, for example, claim to be living at home with their parents. Sometimes they may lose a belonging and misattribute the loss to someone having stolen it. Spatial confusion is often noted to be worse at night; this may be exacerbated by reduced stimulation that would normally assist with orientation.

Perceptual problems may also occur. It is not uncommon for them to fail to recognize their own reflection in a mirror and to think that it is someone else. Similarly, they may misidentify a person close to them and claim that it is a stranger or that although the person appears familiar, he or she is actually a double.

Emotional and personality changes may occur. They may become withdrawn, inert, and apathetic, simply sitting unoccupied, but frequently they may become disinhibited in their behavior, irritable, and verbally aggressive. Insight is lost, so they may fail to acknowledge that there is anything wrong with them. In some cases there may be specific features such as comprehension failure, inappropriate use of language, and recognition failure. They may appear unable to understand what is said to them or to be unable to carry out apparently simple instructions. Language may become incomprehensible with much jargon and many word-finding problems. There may be an inability to name everyday objects or to demonstrate their use. Not uncommonly, objects become misidentified and are used inappropriately. Also frequently apparent will be the inability to carry out everyday actions such as turning a doorknob, buttoning buttons, or other such skills. There may be a difficulty in carrying out daily self-care skills, either because of lack of spontaneity or because the skill itself has apparently been lost. They may put on their clothes in the wrong order and may need help with washing and bathing. Loss of control of bladder function may occur, as may fecal incontinence. Other features may include agitation, restlessness, and wandering.

The characteristics just discussed may not occur in all sufferers of Alzheimer's disease, and as mentioned earlier, there is considerable variation. However, in all cases the disease appears to progress, although the time course is also variable. Generally, younger cases deteriorate more rapidly than older ones. The onset of these signs will depend on the stage of the disorder that suffers have reached.

CAUSES OF ALZHEIMER'S DISEASE

Unfortunately, the short answer to what causes Alzheimer's disease is that no one knows. What is known is that at postmortem, the brain is reduced in weight often to less than 1,000 grams. This marked degree of shrinkage of the brain is accompanied by certain changes in the nerve cells. It is also known that there is a reduction in a chemical that is involved in the production of a neurotransmitter called *acetylcholine*. It is thought that this loss may underlie the disease. Another theory suggests that a slow virus is the cause; it is the case that such a process does underlie another somewhat rarer type of dementia, but there has been no demonstration of a viral cause in Alzheimer's disease. Various substances have been suggested as causes, but the evidence is inconclusive. Currently, there is considerable concern that aluminum may play a major role in the development of Alzheimer's disease. Higher levels of aluminum have been detected in patients with Alzheimer's disease, but this may just be a result of the disease rather than a cause of it. Also, higher incidences of Alzheimer's disease have been reported in areas where there are greater possibilities for the intake of aluminum. Although aluminum may turn out to be an important factor in the incidence of Alzheimer's disease, the evidence can only be considered to suggest this as a possibility at the present time. Other research has suggested a genetic basis to the disease; in some cases it appears to be possible to inherit it—at least some families seem to generate the disorder more than others. However, the mechanism of inheritance, if it exists, is likely to prove complicated.

WHAT TO DO

If you suspect that you have a relative who is suffering from Alzheimer's disease, then the first step is to go to see your physician. This is important because he or she holds the key to many of the services that you might need. Explain exactly what your worries are and ask for your relative to be referred either to a neurologist or to a psychiatrist, preferably one who specializes in old age. A neurologist is a medical consultant who specializes in diseases of the nervous system. He or she will conduct a neurological examination and may also carry out additional diagnostic tests. A psychiatrist is also a medically trained consultant and specializes in the care and treatment of people with mental illness. In many areas there will be psychiatrists who have a particular interest in the psychiatric problems of elderly people; they are often called *psychogeriatricians*. Such psychiatrists tend to work in teams that may include or have access to the services of a clinical psychologist, community psychiatric nurse, social worker, and occupational therapist. The psychiatrist will normally see patients at his or her outpatient clinic, but often it is more useful to have a home visit. Some elderly people will refuse to go to see their doctor because they are unaware that anything is the matter with them. Also, by seeing patients at home, the physician is better able to assess elderly people's ability to manage in a home environment.

The importance of establishing the diagnosis should be stressed because it is quite possible that older people who apparently suffer from confusion or dementia may in fact have a treatable and reversible illness, and a medical specialist will be able to establish this. The psychiatrist may make several recommendations and refer elderly people to other professional people. He or she may, for example, ask the clinical psychologist to carry out a psychological assessment to assist with the diagnosis and establish elderly people's level of functioning. The psychologist may also be able to provide counseling and perhaps suggest ways of managing particular problems. An occupational therapist may be available as well to assist with assessing the everyday skills of elderly people, to advise about any aids and appliances that could be fitted to the home, and perhaps also to advise about activities that may be carried out at home to help keep the elderly person stimulated. The community psychiatric nurse may visit periodically to review any problems and possibly to monitor any medication that has been prescribed. A social worker will often work quite closely with the psychiatrist. The social worker can help in suggesting what is available in the way of day or residential care and can advise about legal matters. From time to time other professionals may become involved, including a physiotherapist or chiropractor. Another important person is a home nurse. He or she can help with various physical problems such as the treatment of varicose ulcers as well as advise on aspects of basic nursing care. Help may also be available to assist patients with dressing, bathing, and washing.

Sometimes the psychiatrist will be able to suggest that patients with Alzheimer's disease attend day care. This may be in a day hospital or day center. The main difference is that a day hospital will have qualified medical and nursing staff available and is a place where medical treatments may therefore be carried out, whereas a day center will not be so staffed. Admission to residential care may sometimes be necessary, and there are various different levels of this. Those with very mild impairment may require nothing more than warden-controlled accommodation, but if independence is further reduced, then residential care may be necessary. In some areas there are rest homes for relatively independent people and nursing homes for those requiring more care and input. The social worker will usually be able to advise about the availability and suitability of these facilities.

Apart from the professional services, there is much good work done by a number of volunteer organizations, the existence of which will vary from one locality to another. Basically they may provide some services together with support, advice, and information.

In summary, the first stage is to obtain an opinion from a suitably qualified medical practitioner and establish what services are available in your area because this varies considerably.

General Management

The finding that patients with dementia present with low levels of acetylcholine led to the optimism that medication aimed at replacing this would alleviate the disorder, slow it down, or even reverse it. Unfortunately, these attempts have not been successful; although research continues, there are as yet no specific treatments available to alter significantly the course of the disease process. Although drugs may be helpful at some points, the general approach at the present time rests largely with management rather than treatment. I now consider the general approach and the management of specific problems.

In Chapter 2 I looked at some of the general aspects of management. Here I discuss the management of more specific problems, but first let me just summarize the general points.

Hopefully the review just presented has shown that many of the behavioral problems encountered occur through no fault of the patients themselves but as a direct result of the effects that the disease has on the brain. First, therefore, difficult though at times it will be, try always to keep this in mind. If patients are being awkward, verbally abusive, uncooperative, or whatever, try not to take this personally.

Second, do not feel that previous standards must be maintained. It is an inevitable result of aging that we become less able to do many of the things that we once did so well. If we are unsteady, we use a walking stick; if our eyesight fails, we wear glasses; and if our hearing lets us down, we may resort to wearing a hearing aid. These are not things to be afraid of or to be ashamed about. For example, in Alzheimer's disease, if patients can no longer use a knife and fork, let them use a spoon.

Third, try to keep a balance. As much as possible, try to maximize their independence. This is good for their morale and motivation and minimizes feelings of guilt that they are a burden. On the other hand, if help is obviously required, then give it. The ideal aim is to assist them in carrying out a particular task by making it a little easier rather than taking it over completely and doing the whole thing for them. All too frequently we are tempted to do too much, either because we find it frustrating to watch somebody else struggling with a particular task or because it is quicker to do it ourselves. Of course, eventually we may need to do virtually everything for them, but we may need to learn how much to do at each particular stage. It is all to do with avoiding extremes.

Fourth, remember that however old and impaired the patients are, they still have the need for some degree of activity and stimulation, to exercise, and so forth. Obviously it is necessary to make some allowance for their degree of impairment, but it is sadly all too common to visit an old people's home and see all of the residents sitting unoccupied. Many psychological studies have shown that elderly people, even if they are impaired, are likely to function at a better level if they take part in some activity and exercise moderately. Simple activities can be arranged, even if it is only doing a small jigsaw puzzle, making Christmas cards, or doing a bit of indoor gardening. Exploit any previous hobbies they once had and may still be able to do to some extent. In other cases previous hobbies might be simplified to bring the hobbies within their range of capability. Music is a useful source of stimulation, and even very demented people will show some response to old favorite tunes. Pets provide enormous comfort and are a relaxation in themselves. Exercise may take the form of simple nonstrenuous keep-fit movements or a walk out in the fresh air.

Memory and Orientation

I have already noted that memory loss and disorientation are central features of Alzheimer's disease and that they are at the root of various other behavioral problems. Psychologists usually make a distinction between different types of memory. *Short-term memory* refers to the ability to retain something for just a few seconds. It allows us to, for example, retain a telephone number just long enough to dial it. Patients with Alzheimer's disease may have some impair-

ment in this type of memory, and they may be very susceptible to the effects of distraction. Try to make sure that information is given to them in small amounts—just a few words
at a time— and allow them to respond before giving them
any more. Repeat the information as necessary. *Long-term
memory*, as the term implies, is required in order to remember things from hour to hour, day to day. This sort of memory
is very impaired in patients with Alzheimer's disease, so it is
important to repeat information many times. Very long-term
memory, or remote memory, eventually becomes impaired
too, but there is a tendency for older memories to be more
resilient. Patients may be able to say something about their
early life yet be quite unable to remember what happened
only yesterday.

Many professionals and centers concerned with the care
of the elderly commonly use a technique called *reality orientation* (RO). This form of therapy, and other related approaches, is described in detail by Holden and Woods (1988).
Perhaps to call it a technique is not quite accurate, for it is
really a whole approach or philosophy to working with elderly people who have memory impairments. RO is not, of
course, aimed at curing the memory loss; rather the approach attempts to compensate for it and, if possible, to
keep elderly people in touch with current events as far as
practicable.

There are two types of RO: 24-hour RO and formal RO.
As the name implies, 24-hour RO involves the active reorien-
tation of elderly people by ensuring that every time someone
interacts with them, relevant information is given about
time, place, and current activity. This means doing or saying
something that attempts to concentrate patients' attention
on some aspect of current reality. Ideally, patients are verbally provided with information about the time, day, month,
year, and so forth; where they are; what they are doing; and
what is happening as often as possible. Of course, because of
the memory impairment, the procedure needs to be repetitive and carried out on a continuing basis. The aim is to tactfully correct confused behavior when it occurs. However,
care must be taken to avoid confrontation or direct contra-

diction, as this will often make matters worse. More appropriate action would be to distract or divert their attention onto something that is real and of current relevance. When correct behavior does occur, it should be encouraged and praised. This is often easier said than done, and using this approach does not necessarily make the task any easier. However, what it does do is provide a structured way of working with elderly memory-impaired people.

A second very important part of 24-hour RO is to ensure that there are plenty of orientation aids available. We all rely on clocks to tell us what the time is and calendars or newspapers to tell us the date or day. We all have to use signposts when visiting a town for the first time. For memory-impaired older people, even routine day-to-day life may become unfamiliar. They may find it difficult to remember how to find the bathroom. Try to make sure that there are clocks, calendars, and notices around the home that clearly display the necessary information and keep encouraging them to make use of such aids. Leave large, clearly written notes in prominent places to remind them to carry out particular tasks.

In many day centers and day hospitals, the staff use formal RO. The following is a method for doing RO in groups: Small groups meet with one or two therapists and the group focuses on specific orientation information with the use of various aids such as a clock, calendar, or weather chart. This sort of procedure can be carried out at home. Perhaps 10 or 15 minutes can be set aside each day. During this time patients may be encouraged to rehearse the day, month, and year; talk about the weather; and be shown a newspaper and talk about the main headlines. Rehearsal of information takes place in an attempt to improve retention of it.

A related approach is called *reminiscence therapy,* which is a method used in many centers for elderly people. Reminiscence essentially refers to the recollection of past memories and is something we all do from time to time. However, reminiscence does not involve the recollection of simply any memory. If we stop for a moment and allow ourselves to freely reminisce, we are likely to bring to mind memories of particularly personal events rather than factual or, for want of a better word, unemotional ones. Such memories may be of happy childhood times, just odd images of particular occurrences that may pop up for no obvious reason and not necessarily major events that marked some important turning point in our lives. Interestingly, though, our memories are anything but accurate accounts of what actually happened, and so our reminiscences are unique reconstructions of past personal experiences. The memories we recall will have undergone embellishment and elaboration. They will rarely be accurate records of what actually happened. Reminiscence by older people is often seen as a negative consequence of old age and therefore something that perhaps ought not to be encouraged. This is exemplified by references to older people living in the past. Obsessive rumination about past failures may not be very healthy; for many elderly people, however, reminiscence can form the basis of useful interaction, for many memories, although being unique and personal, will be about the same general experiences of many, such as World War II. Reminiscence therefore facilitates communication between very different sorts of people who may have little more in common with one another than their experiences of public events.

Because older people often retain some memory of their earlier life, this residual ability can be used sometimes with good effect. A useful way of encouraging reminiscence is to give elderly people old photographs of them and their family, old musical tunes to listen to, and pictures of their home town as it used to be and as it is now. Older people are reminded all too often about their failures and limitations; for this reason, reminiscence is seen as a valuable way of enhancing self-esteem because it focuses on residual abilities rather than current failings. As I have noted, reminiscence facilitates interaction, not just between one elderly person and another, but between young and old. Grandchildren are interested in hearing about a world of horse-drawn vehicles, steam locomotives, and war experiences and can learn much about modern history this way. This in turn gives older people some feeling of usefulness and pleasure in making others happy. For most children there is always something almost magical about grandparents, and belonging to an earlier era is part of this. Psychologists have also suggested that reminiscence plays an important part in the life-review process so that it facilitates the resolution of past problems and allows these to be seen in perspective. Reminiscence is therefore a useful approach to caring for elderly people. It is likely to prove enjoyable for all concerned.

For people with Alzheimer's disease, reminiscence therapy is likely to take a more simple and structured form because this disorder tends to reduce spontaneity and initiative. Any materials used will clearly need to be comprehensible to them. Words or pictures that cannot be understood will be of no use, but even fairly severely impaired people will respond to stimulation at some level, such as a familiar tune or sensation. It may be necessary to help them to respond by prompting them.

If you take on the care of an older person you do not know very well, then reminiscence is a very useful way of learning more about that person and understanding his or her uniqueness and behavior within a historical context. As I have noted, it can be an enjoyable and rewarding experience for both. This is very important because often one hears that there seems little point in being old or that there is little satisfaction in looking after an older person. One value of reminiscence is that it makes such work interesting and worthwhile, and it allows us to see the elderly person as a unique person. This should assist in facilitating a relationship between caregiver and elderly person.

What is the evidence that these approaches are effective? The effects of RO seem to be fairly modest and specific. Patients may show some improvement in orientation, but nothing spectacular, and the improvement does not reliably generalize to other aspects of their memory or behavior. Improvement tends to be limited to what has been rehearsed. The effects are not maintained either, so the method has to be used continuously. However, some psychological studies seem to suggest that patients receiving RO may also show some improvement in mood. The limited effects of RO may seem a little disconcerting, but bear in mind that the approach is being used in the face of a progressive disease superimposed on the aging process and so in some way is analogous to walking up an escalator that is coming down. If one can slow down the process or make life more comfortable, then this must surely mean that the approach is worth taking. Viewed in this way, RO is certainly not a waste of time, although obviously it does involve some concerted effort for limited benefit.

Reminiscence therapy may be viewed in a similar light. There is no conclusive evidence that it significantly alters the behavior of elderly people, but intuitively it seems worthwhile because it permits them to realize that they can still do something well, it is enjoyable, and it creates a richer environment for them, which must be a good thing.

Wandering

Wandering is one of the most difficult problems presented by people with Alzheimer's disease, especially if it occurs at night. Because people who wander are potentially at risk, it causes a permanent source of stress to the caregivers.

There are many possible causes of wandering. Physical discomfort of some kind may cause it, such as pain or constipation. Disorientation may contribute to the behavior because confused elderly people may be trying to find some clue as to their whereabouts and identity. They may be searching for a lost belonging or trying to find the way to the bathroom. Misidentification of their surroundings or belief that they are somewhere else can similarly be responsible. It is not unusual for elderly people to wander out of the house at 5 p.m. in the belief that they are on their way home from work! Restless or agitated behavior may result from depression or boredom. It is by no means unusual to find that those who wander are people who once did a lot of walking or traveling. Wandering may be worse at night because of the reduction in stimulation, which tends to worsen disorientation. The first step, then, is to try to identify the cause of wandering.

If you are persuading wandering people to return, it is better to avoid any confrontation or direct contradiction. Try to tactfully persuade them that there is something much more interesting for them to do at home. As a precaution, it is not a bad idea to get them to carry some form of conspicuous identity. It may be necessary to install new locks or bolts on the door that are difficult to operate. An alternative possibility is to install a bell or similar device that operates when the door is opened. It may also help to ensure that lighting is adequate and bright and to leave a light on at night. Medication may be used, but really as a last resort, as most of the relevant medications can make the confusion even worse.

Sleep

As people get older they need less sleep. They tend to wake more often during the night and perhaps to wake earlier in the morning. Older people also often take catnaps during the day and may exercise little. All this adds up to possible sleep problems. Try to keep them awake during the day and keep them as active as possible. Avoid putting them to bed too early and ensure that they have visited the bathroom before retiring. Leaving on a landing light, and perhaps one in the bathroom too, may be a good idea. Medication may sometimes be necessary because it is important that you sleep too.

Incontinence

Another very difficult problem is incontinence. Urinary incontinence may occur during the day or the night, although the latter is more common in the earlier stage. There are many possible causes of incontinence. Infection and prostate problems are among the possible physical causes. Constipation may cause incontinence, and this should be prevented by exercise, a high-fiber diet, adequate fluids, and if necessary, the general practitioner may prescribe laxatives. It is therefore a good idea to have a doctor check for any physical abnormalities. Psychological causes may include forgetting where the bathroom is, being unable to get there in time, being unable to undress and dress, failing to recognize the bathroom, or being unable to control the bladder. It is a good plan to regularly remind them to go to the lavatory every 2 hours, supervising as necessary, and perhaps waking them once or twice at night. It may be useful to find out if there is a continence adviser in the area. An occupational therapist may be able to advise about useful bathroom aids.

Verbal Abuse

As I have already said, try to remember that verbal abuse is something that may come as part of the disease and is not deliberately intended. Patients may be accusing and suspicious, which can be upsetting and embarrassing. Verbal abuse and accusations sometimes occur because they have lost something and misattributed this to someone having stolen or hidden it. Try to ignore such remarks and avoid getting into confrontation situations or arguments. Try to ensure purposeful involvement, stimulation, and activity. Try to remain relaxed and speak calmly. Hallucinations sometimes occur in Alzheimer's disease, and patients may "see" other people in the room or develop the delusion that, for example, someone is in the attic. It is not advisable to directly contradict these claims, but try to sympathize with them and to calm them down. Concentrate on trying to convey that you are empathetic and that you care about and are listening to what they are saying. Respond more to their distress than to the actual content of what they are saying. Occasionally they might be aggressive or violent. Fortunately, they usually calm down quickly and rapidly forget about it. Try to stay calm and avoid getting involved and making the matter worse. Try to identify what it was that triggered the episode and avoid it the next time. However, these situations are likely to lead to considerable emotional reaction in the caregiver and it may help to call a professional or friend for support.

Self-Care

Try to avoid doing too much for the elderly person but provide just enough prompting and supervision. An occupational therapist can advise about and supply a variety of eating, bathing, and dressing aids. There are many such aids that make eating easier and different fastenings that simplify dressing. Make meals that are easy to eat and that require a minimum of manipulation.

Relocation

There are differing views about day care for elderly people with dementia. One view is that a new environment will make the disorientation more troublesome and that it is better to maintain confused people in familiar surroundings. However, this does not take into account the stress placed on the caregiver. These factors have to be balanced against each other.

Elderly people may be reluctant to go at first, but it is worth persevering in persuading them to go because this may be a useful source of stimulation for them and a much needed break for you.

It is true that when we get older, we are less keen to consider major changes in our life, and moving back home is a major change. However, as with most things in life, it is largely a question of balance. The main factors in the equation are your relative's health and your own health. Residential care may well be the only realistic answer.

If elderly people are clearly no longer able to care for themselves, if the necessary support is not available, or if you are simply unable to cope any longer, then residential care may be a necessity. Do not feel guilty—you can only do so much and if your own health suffers, then you will need help as well. Guilt is a perfectly natural feeling in these situations, of course, but sometimes a move is inevitable and it is nothing to be ashamed of.

Of course, when possible, admission to some kind of residential care should be planned and thoroughly discussed beforehand, and there should be opportunity for considerable preparation. Any kind of move is likely to be disrupting to some extent, especially if it involves giving up independence, which it usually does. On the one hand, residential care can provide security through having a structure, but the difficulty often comes in there being only one standard or set of rules. This may mean that for some, too much is done, a point that is worth reemphasizing. It is important to try to find the right sort of place, and this may be a long task. Factors likely to minimize the disruption of such a move include elderly people being able to take at least some of their belongings, furniture, ornaments, and so on with them. They will then be surrounded by familiar things, and this will help them to feel more at home and more in control of their lives. In the case of a nursing home or residential home, there is no reason for the place not to have a reasonably homelike atmosphere, and no home should ever smell of incontinence—any well-trained nurse will tell you that this need never be the case. Remember, too, that for many older people, the local hospital may be remembered as a workhouse (a house of corrections) and this stigma can be difficult to eradicate. Anyone who has been in hospital will know that one may feel quite insecure there. It is a rather barren environment where one has to do what others dictate, often without sufficient explanation or reassurance, and it is rather different from the secure home environment. We associate hospitals with places where we go for a short time to get better, but older people may fear that they will never get better and so may be frightened that they will never leave the hospital. Sadly, one often experiences immense inertia if one suggests that perhaps a few simple changes could make a ward seem more homelike and friendly. Yet this is very important, for if elderly people become long-stay patients, then the hospital is their home, but few would choose to live in a hospital environment.

Looking After Yourself

Caring for a person with Alzheimer's disease is one of the greatest stresses of our time, as any caregiver will testify. The problems are considerable, their management difficult, and the demands seem to go on forever. This means that it is essential to devise some way of obtaining some relief, even temporarily, from the problem. The first thing to do is to ensure that you are in contact with the local professional and volunteer services. They have had experience with these situations and are there to help. So do not feel that taking advantage of what is offered is accepting charity, and do not wait until you are at the end of your tether and can no longer cope. Accepting help, or even resorting to residential care for your relative, is not a sign of failure. Everyone involved in the business of caring for elderly people knows well enough what you are going through, and recognizing in yourself when you need help is a strength, not a weakness.

Obtaining temporary relief from the problem can come in different ways. If you are lucky you may have another relative or a friend who can pop in one or two afternoons a week to keep an eye on your relative so that you can go out for a while. In some areas there may be a "granny-sitting service" that trains volunteers to be available for this purpose. There may be a day hospital that your relative can attend on certain days. This might not sound like a great deal of time, but you will find it an enormous help just to have those few hours to yourself.

In some areas there may be a holiday relief bed in a local home for the elderly people, nursing home, or hospital. This is a good idea because it will often be the only way that you are going to get a holiday to yourself. Taking your relative on holiday is not generally considered a good idea because this can add to the problems resulting from his or her confusion and so it will hardly be a holiday for you.

All of these services may or may not be locally available, but asking your physician or a psychiatrist who specializes in the care of elderly people is the place to start. Again, do not feel guilty about the need to take a break. Everyone needs to do this at some time, especially if they are caring for someone 24 hours a day. No person can tolerate endless amounts of stress. Knowing that you can have a break will give you the strength to carry on a bit further; if all you can see ahead is no end to the situation, then the stress is made even worse. After a short break or holiday you will feel relieved and refreshed and feel able to resume your task.

From time to time throughout this book, I refer to the importance of learning to cope with caring for another person. In general, caregivers should ensure that they set limits clearly, so that the person for whom they are caring understands what the boundaries are. It is important to attend to your own health, for if this suffers you will find it more difficult to provide care. Try to develop an insight into the person's needs—imagine being in their position—and try to be tolerant, empathic, nonjudgmental, and understanding, but ensure that your own needs are being met as well. There is one additional thing that you must do: Learn to deal with anxiety and tension. In chapter 7 I look specifically at stress management and some simple methods that you can learn and practice regularly.

A question that caregivers often ask is the length of time they will have to look after an elderly demented relative. Unfortunately, this is not easy to answer. It depends on many factors, such as the age of onset and the type of dementia. A rough estimate would perhaps be 7–8 years, but that is only an average figure and it tells nothing about the individual case.

As is clear from this chapter, our current knowledge of dementia is very limited. To some extent it is a problem to which medical research has addressed itself only in recent years, and it is a very complex one. There is little doubt that the numbers of people suffering from dementia will continue to increase over the next few decades, simply because there is a continuing increase in the number of older people, especially those over the age of 80 and, as I have shown, the incidence of Alzheimer's disease increases with age. As yet, there is no convincing theory of Alzheimer's disease and no curative treatment.

REFERENCES AND FURTHER READING

Miller, E. (1977). *Abnormal ageing.* Chichester, England: Wiley.

Holden, U., & Woods, R. T. (1988). *Reality orientation: Psychological approaches to the "confused" elderly.* Edinburgh, Scotland: Churchill Livingstone.

5

Stroke

Disorders affecting the blood vessels of the brain are, unfortunately, not uncommon. With the exception of heart disease and cancer, they are still one of the most common causes of death. Once referred to as apoplexy, a stroke (or *cerebrovascular accident* as it is medically termed) can cause a wide variety of symptoms; although often seen in older people, strokes can occur in young people as well. However, the probability of having a stroke tends to increase with age. One large survey found that people between 75 and 79 were three times more likely to suffer a stroke than those aged between 65 and 69.

When the blood supply to the brain is disrupted in some way, oxygen and glucose fail to reach the areas served by the blood vessel in question. Under such conditions the nerve cells in the brain can survive only for a limited time, and normally once they die they cannot grow again. The two main types of stroke are called *intracranial hemorrhage* and *cerebral ischemia*. An intracranial hemorrhage may be either intracerebral, which means that the hemorrhage is in the brain itself, or it may be a subarachnoid. The latter occurs in the subarachnoid space, which is the area under the very thin covering of the brain and its blood vessels.

An intracranial hemorrhage can occur when a weakness in the wall of a blood vessel causes it to blow up like a balloon. This is called an *aneurysm*. The aneurysm may rupture, causing a hemorrhage. There may be no warning, although sometimes people may experience symptoms such as headache and nausea beforehand. The extent of damage obviously depends on the size of the hemorrhage. If severe, death may occur, but smaller hemorrhages may cause limited damage and loss of ability.

The other main type of stroke occurs when a blood vessel becomes blocked by a fatty deposit. The resulting dead area is called an *area of infarction*. Sometimes this type of stroke occurs suddenly, but it may take time to develop fully. On occasions "ministrokes" may occur first, and these may last only momentarily or for a few hours. Because the blockage may only be temporary, damage and subsequent loss of ability may be minimal. However, some residual mild degree of impairment is the rule.

There is no reason to assume that people who have had a stroke will necessarily have another one, but in some cases repeated strokes may occur. In such instances, however, the stroke may be in a different part of the brain. When a stroke has been associated with hypertension (high blood pressure), medication can be given to reduce this in order to decrease the probability of another stroke.

Following a stroke people may lose consciousness, and when they awaken they may be confused, disoriented, and appear to be intellectually impaired. Probably the most familiar result of a stroke is hemiplegia (paralysis of one side of the body). There may be poor concentration and memory, and irritability; their mood may fluctuate easily, and they may tire easily. This is referred to as the *acute stage*, when recovery is most rapid.

RECOVERY

Recovery is something of an inappropriate term because it implies regaining a previous level of ability completely. Such complete recovery, from what I have already said, would be optimistic in the majority of cases. What I am discussing here is the extent to which people may show improvement after a stroke. As a rule of thumb, about one third of stroke victims die within 1 month, approximately another third make a complete or near-complete recovery, and the remainder are left with considerable residual disability.

It is useful to be aware of how much recovery can be expected, what one can expect to recover, what factors influence recovery, and over what period of time one can expect recovery to continue. In addition, it is important to establish what can be done to help facilitate recovery and to support residual functioning.

Surprisingly little is known about the natural processes of recovery. It is very difficult to be sure about recovery rates because it depends to a large extent on what one is measuring and how one measures it. Recovery will also depend on the nature of the brain damage and to what extent other areas of the brain that are undamaged can take over the lost role. However, there seems to be general agreement that recovery after brain damage tends to proceed at a faster rate in the earlier stages before eventually reaching a plateau. Recovery from speech impairment, for example, has been found to be more rapid in the first 3 months or so and then to level off.

Another factor influencing recovery is age. For example, younger patients with speech impairment tend to show a better recovery than older ones, although the difference is not great.

The cause of speech impairment also seems to influence outcome. Recovery from speech impairment resulting from head injury, for instance, tends to be better than that caused by a stroke. Recovery also tends to be better in milder cases of speech impairment, and patients with difficulty in speech expression do better. Outcome is poorer if patients have global speech impairment (i.e., both comprehension and expression problems). The terms *global* and *expressive* refer to the classification often adopted for speech disorders. In expressive speech disorders, the defect may only be a mild word-finding difficulty, but it ranges to complete loss of speech. The other major type of speech impairment involves difficulty in understanding the spoken word. More often than not, however, these deficits coexist. Recovery may be further influenced by handedness, and left-handed people with speech impairments seem to recover better than right-handed ones.

In the case of memory impairments less is known about recovery, but this does seem to depend on where the damage has occurred. Although complete recovery would be the exception, if it occurs at all, some patients do show improvement for up to a year afterwards; it is not unknown for others to continue to improve after this time.

Given that a certain amount of recovery can take place, what can account for this? There are basically three theories discussed by Miller (1984). The first type of theory suggests that two things happen: The first is that there is damage to a certain part of the brain that is centrally involved in a particular function but that in addition to this, there is damage to other parts of the brain that are not so centrally involved in that function. It is proposed that only the second type of damage is reversible. This theory would explain some degree of apparent recovery in some patients, although the basic deficit, be it speech, memory, or whatever, remains. It is postulated that such temporary damage might be due to edema (swelling) that subsides with time.

A second theory of recovery proposes that when a particular function is lost due to damage to a particular part of the brain, another area may take over the lost function. There is some evidence that this may occur in very young children, although it has not been shown for older people. Very young children who sustain damage to the speech areas of the left side of the brain have nevertheless been reported to learn to speak, presumably because the right side of the brain has been able to take over this particular function.

The third main theory of recovery makes no assumptions about the recovery of a particular function, but proposes that patients may be able to learn to do a particular task in a different way. This theory would seem to be a better explanation of recovery because it can explain permanent deficits but with the ability to circumvent these in some cases.

Having said something briefly about recovery, what can one expect from active intervention? There are two possible goals: One is to help patients regain their lost ability and the other is to teach them alternative ways of performing a particular function. Less ambitious, but often more realistic, is to accept that neither of these works in some cases and that the goal therefore has to be to capitalize on the patients' residual capabilities.

Trying to help people regain a lost ability is the hardest goal to attain because therapeutic interventions of a psychological kind would not seem likely to have any effect on the brain damage itself and hence little effect on the deficit itself. However, it is by no means unreasonable to propose that psychological methods might help in teaching patients how to get around the problem by using an alternative strategy. One may take as an example a case of someone suffering from a memory impairment. At the present time there are no treatments that would allow restoration of the person's memory; therefore, if the person's memory failure is due to information simply not being laid down properly in the brain, then one possible therapeutic goal would be to teach the person how to use external memory aids. A limitation of intervention of this kind concerns its generalizability. In many cases a strategy for getting around one particular problem may be useless in helping with a similar problem in a different situation. So, for example, if a person goes out shopping but forgets what he or she went there for, a shopping list will help, but making lists is not likely to be very practical as a way of compensating for forgetting people's names or faces or remembering to do a particular thing at a particular time.

With any intervention it should be recognized that in many cases, any gains are unlikely to be spectacular but will be at best modest. Nevertheless, such modest improvements must be better than nothing at all and may at least help the person to view life more positively.

Another factor to be considered is that intervention in the early stages is likely to be more effective than if left until later. At first sight it may appear that this is because the natural spontaneous recovery processes are faster in the early stages, but even allowing for this it seems that early intervention produces better results. This certainly seems to be true in physical rehabilitation. If physiotherapy begins early, then contractures of muscles can be reduced, whereas once this has occurred, it becomes much more difficult to treat the patient.

I have already shown that age can affect recovery, although such age effects are not drastically large. It has been found that in the case of recovery from speech impairment, for example, elderly people may show the same degree of improvement as middle-age people.

Other factors that need to be considered are motivation, personality, and insight. Obviously patients who lack insight into their disability are less likely to be motivated to improve it. People overwhelmed by the sudden and severe aspect of their loss may become withdrawn and depressed. This will also clearly interfere with motivation and response to rehabilitation.

MANAGEMENT

Having said something about recovery and intervention generally, I now look at strategies for some particular problems. Recall from the previous discussion that there are three possible goals: attempting to reinstate lost abilities, teaching new ways of circumventing the problem, and concentrating on utilizing residual skills. Most of the following section is based on the assumption that teaching alternative ways of achieving a goal is more realistic than attempting to reinstate lost abilities. However, attention should always be given to the development of residual capabilities. In this chapter I focus primarily on psychological aspects. However, readers will be aware, stroke often leads to loss of physical function. Detailed discussion of physical management is beyond the scope of this book, and a physiotherapist will be able to advise on this aspect of rehabilitation. I give some specific examples later when I discuss memory problems, but here I should mention the importance of making a list of patients' previous interests, hobbies, and occupations, including those in which they have expressed an interest but for one reason or another have never taken any further. Then make a list of the skills needed to carry these out and consider which of these patients still retain. Do not worry how trivial it appears to you. Even if they can only perform a tiny part of a task, that will be better than doing nothing at all. Often an occupational therapist will be able to visit and, as well as giving advice about aids that can be fitted in the home to help compensate for functional losses in stroke victims, may also be able to advise about suitable activities for patients. There may also be a stroke support group that they can attend. These are often run by volunteers.

The general approach is in many ways the same as for other disorders occurring in old age. Essentially one needs to remember that stroke patients have the same general needs as everyone else: purposeful and organized activity, stimulation, a sense of purpose, emotional fulfillment, exercise, social activity, and so on. In addition, they have certain individual special needs.

The starting point is usually dealing with the psychological reaction to the effects of the stroke. Almost by definition the onset of a stroke is sudden and the effects are quite variable. The effect of a stroke will depend on its size and the area of the brain affected. Some strokes, as noted earlier, cause few symptoms, whereas others produce severe impairments. A broad range of deficits may occur in intellect, attention, concentration, memory, movement, speech, emotion, personality, and everyday skills.

When considering emotional problems it is not always easy to establish whether they are due to the brain damage itself, to the problems adjusting to the effects of the damage, or to a combination of the two. However, it is known that patients with damage to the left side of the brain are more likely to be depressed. On the other hand, severity of depression depends on the severity of brain damage. Generally, greater degrees of depression can be expected in patients with greater intellectual and physical impairments, but as many as 40% of patients who have suffered a stroke may present some degree of depression.

People who become depressed will have difficulty motivating themselves to do things. Therefore I examine ways of improving motivation. First, then, I discuss behavioral management.

BEHAVIORAL MANAGEMENT

Behavioral methods of management, sometimes referred to as *behavior therapy* and *behavior modification*, consist of a series of techniques applied systematically to increase the probability of some behavior occurring or to decrease it. I have already touched on this approach to management, but here I briefly restate the general principles. When I use the word *behavior* I am referring to any action shown by patients. It does not specifically refer to desirable or undesirable behavior but to the action or activity itself.

In the case of stroke patients, they may need to be motivated to participate in a rehabilitation program or just to carry out residual skills. On the other hand, there may be a perceived need to try to decrease or eliminate their negative or depressive thoughts. I discussed this in the chapter on depression.

As previously mentioned, the basic technique used to encourage a particular behavior is referred to as *reinforcement*. Behavior is more likely to recur if it leads to a pleasant outcome or is rewarded. When a behavior has been rewarded, it has been reinforced. If an unpleasant outcome results from a behavior, then people tend not to repeat it, or at least to be less likely to do so. Although something of an oversimplification, the behavior of many stroke patients can be understood in this way. They may avoid speaking if their speech is impaired, for example, because the outcome may be unpleasant. Other people may be unable to understand them or think that they are drunk or abnormal. It is a reminder that they are no longer able to perform what was once such a simple action for them, one they took for granted. This may lead to loss of motivation to participate in social activities. Furthermore, stroke patients may be reluctant to take part in a rehabilitation program because every attempt made leads to failure on a particular task that once seemed so easy it may even have been completely automatic. Patients' negative thoughts can also be understood in this way. Patients may tell themselves that they are a failure because their impairments interfere with so many of their activities. In summary, then, stroke patients' tendencies to avoid situations or withdraw from them can be understood in psychological terms because the outcome is always unfavourable and nonreinforcing for them. A moment's reflection will allow us to see that this holds true for everyone: If something we do has a pleasant outcome, then we tend to repeat it; if it leads to an unpleasant outcome, we are less likely to do it again.

How, then, do we apply behavioral management techniques to stroke victims? Clearly, we need to ensure that when we ask them to carry out a certain task that it leads to a rewarding outcome. First, great emphasis must be placed on the value of positive reinforcement and rewarding opportunities in encouraging patients to make some effort toward a specific rehabilitation goal. Social reinforcement, praise, encouragement, or simply giving them attention are effective forms of rewarding behavior. Second, we need to ensure that the rehabilitation goal is divided up into a number of small stages. This makes it easier for them to succeed and minimizes failure. Motivation will therefore improve. The first step must always be within their potential capability, and it is no use proceeding to the next step before the previous one has been accomplished. Reward must then be given immediately. It does not matter how minimal the first step appears. Even a slight achievement is better than nothing.

SPEECH IMPAIRMENTS

Speech impairments are, of course, one of the most common impairments to result from a stroke. A speech therapist will usually be able to assess patients and, where appropriate, devise a suitable treatment program. When the impairment is very severe, it may be possible to teach patients to use an alternative method of communication, such as a letter board or a sheet marked out into small squares in which each square contains a picture of the idea to be expressed that can be pointed to. There are also various types of electronic communication devices that will produce a printed output.

MEMORY

It is not uncommon for stroke victims to suffer from some degree of memory impairment. Some patients may appear to have poor memory because they have difficulty with attention and concentration and hence never take in the information properly. In other cases there may be a basic deficit in actually recording the memory in the brain. In others there may be a retrieval failure. However, in practice it is often difficult to know which of these is the problem or whether there is a combination of problems.

Complete memory loss is actually rare in stroke victims unless there has been considerable generalized brain damage. Many patients retain a wide range of learning skills. Provided that they are intellectually intact, memory-disordered patients have, for instance, been taught how to use computer language, to operate a computer, to learn shorthand, and to learn new musical tunes. This may be the case even if patients cannot remember what happened yesterday or cannot remember learning the skill itself. These skills can all be learned with repetitive practice, which leads to them being carried out in an automatic way. It is only when the task requires some memory for the learning event itself that problems occur.

Diaries and daily timetables are potentially useful because they store information about what patients have to do at certain times. Successful use of a diary can enable them to remember things to do and to keep appointments. Lists and plans can be displayed in prominent places.

Such external stores of information compensate for patients with forgetfulness, provided they remember to use them. But having a diary or timetable is of no use if they do not remember to consult it regularly. In the years to come it is likely that some kind of electronic memory aid will be developed, but devices of this kind are currently complicated or cumbersome. An alternative approach is to combine a simple timer with a diary. Patients then only have to learn that when they hear the alarm, which is preset to ring at relevant times, they need to consult their diary or timetable.

Some readers may believe that memory improves with practice, rather like exercising. Unfortunately, this is not the case, and memory can only be improved by learning more efficient strategies for storing and retrieving information. One such strategy is called the PQRST technique. I outlined this in chapter 1 and so do not discuss it here.

Mental imagery is another technique that has been taught to patients with memory difficulties. Typically, these methods have been used to help people remember other people's names. I outlined the techniques in chapter 1. Patients suffering from memory impairment as a result of a stroke have shown improved ability to learn people's names using this method.

REFERENCES AND FURTHER READING

Miller, E. (1984). *Recovery and management of neuropsychological impairments.* Chichester, England: Wiley.

Walsh, K. (1988). *Neuropsychology: A clinical approach.* Edinburgh, Scotland: Churchill Livingstone.

6

Other Conditions

So far, I have considered anxiety, depression, dementia, and stroke. These are relatively more common in old age, but there are other conditions that can occur in elderly people. In this chapter I consider some of these. However, this chapter is somewhat shorter because in most of these conditions, people are likely to be admitted to hospital because of special treatment needs. Home caregivers are therefore less likely to be involved in the acute management of these conditions.

ACUTE CONFUSIONAL STATES

The term *acute confusional state* is probably self-explanatory. *Acute* refers to the relatively sudden onset. *Confusional* refers to the confused appearance of people's behavior and their lack of coherence and clarity of thinking. *State* implies that there is something temporary about the condition. Thus, the term refers to a period of confusion that starts suddenly and is potentially of limited duration. In other words, unlike dementia, an acute confusional state is reversible. The acute confusional state is sometimes referred to as delirium. Having said this, though, acute confusional states may also occur in people who also show some evidence of dementia. Although not unique to elderly people and also occurring in young people, older people are particularly susceptible to these conditions. As already noted, the onset is sudden, in contrast to dementia where the onset is more gradual. People in an acute confusional state become frightened, disoriented, and confused in speech and behavior. This confusion tends to be worse at night. They may experience visual hallucinations that are often improbable, such as "seeing" children in the room or small figures dancing on the window sill. Because of these hallucinations and the fear they induce, the acutely confused people's behavior may be unpredictable, erratic, and aggressive.

Acute confusional states are most commonly caused by underlying medical conditions, and the recovery will depend on the nature and severity of these. Such conditions include infections (often the chest or urinary tract); toxicities (most often drugs or alcohol); dehydration; metabolic disturbances (usually associated with vitamin deficiency); malfunctioning of an organ (e.g., heart condition); or condition involving the brain (e.g., a stroke). The position can be complicated by the fact that, as already mentioned, people suffering from an acute confusional state may already have some degree of dementia. Acute confusional states are sometimes seen in elderly people living alone who have become depressed or physically disabled and because of this they have stopped eating and drinking. Older people are very sensitive to the effects of drugs, especially in combination, and they require smaller doses of many of these. Clearly, if the underlying medical condition is serious, then the outcome will be poor, but where treatment can be offered, the recovery will be good with a minimal degree of residual impairment.

It may be possible in many cases for relatives to care for acutely confused people at home, but this may be difficult because if left alone they may wander, refuse to take medication, and so on. Admission to the hospital may then be necessary, either to a general hospital if special care needs to be given to the medical condition or to a psychiatric unit if behavior is very disturbed. In either event, treatment for the medical condition will be given, together with nursing care; in other respects the general approach will be similar to that described for dementia.

Because of hallucinations and disorientation acutely confused people will tend to misinterpret incoming information. This may be more so if there is poor lighting or if they are surrounded by strange people in a strange place. They should therefore be treated calmly and with reassurance. Lighting should be clear and bright enough, and surroundings should be made as familiar as possible. Communication should be clear and simple, and the caregiver should use short, straightforward words and sentences, repeating these as necessary.

It is important to try to get acutely confused people to take in plenty of fluids, especially if dehydration is present. Vitamin tablets or injections may be advised if they have not been eating because vitamin deficiency, if not the actual cause, may exacerbate the condition.

If they are lying in bed or are otherwise immobile, it will be necessary to prevent pressure sores by turning them to a different position at 2-hour intervals. Soft bed socks will help prevent such sores on the feet.

Incontinence may occur, so if they are very confused it may be necessary to assist them to the lavatory. Taking them to the bathroom at 2-hour intervals will help minimize incontinence. Constipation may later lead to fecal incontinence, and plenty of fluids will help prevent this.

It they are very agitated and restless the doctor may prescribe a low dose of a suitable drug, but physical restraint should be avoided because this will make confused and frightened people even more so.

FUNCTIONAL PSYCHOTIC CONDITIONS

The term *psychotic* refers to a class of disorders characterized by a disturbance in people's perception of reality. The term would thus include the "organic" disorders already discussed. *Organic* refers to a disorder that can be clearly related to underlying changes in the nervous system, as opposed to the term *functional,* which is used to describe conditions that have not yet been shown to have a definite underlying physical cause. Such organic disorders, as with acute confusional states and dementia, may include delusions and hallucinations, but these phenomena can occur in certain functional disorders too. Delusions and hallucinations are not in themselves disorders, but they are used as signs in the diagnosis of psychiatric disorders. Bearing this in mind, I now consider them in more detail under separate headings.

Delusions

Delusions may be described as false and unshakable beliefs, and they may be of different types. Delusions of grandeur may occur, and in these instances individuals may believe that they have superior capabilities. Delusions of persecution can also occur; in these cases people become overly suspicious, such that they may misattribute various behaviors and utterances as being directed toward them in a destructive way. In severe depression delusions are usually negative in content, so that people may believe that they have become destitute, that their insides are rotting away, and so on. In another condition, called *hypomania,* which is fairly uncommon in older people, people become extremely overactive in behavior and euphoric in mood and may believe that they are capable of incredible feats of achievement. Appetite and sleep tend to be poor, as in depression. As noted previously, hypomania can alternate with depression in manic-depressive psychosis, although it is more common for one or the other condition to prevail. If severe bouts of depression, hypomania, or both have been a lifelong pattern, there tends to be a family history of this, although this is less likely to be true if it occurs for the first time in old age. The condition can be treated with drugs, although it may be necessary for them to take these regularly on an ongoing basis.

In yet another condition, called *paraphrenia,* the delusions may be of a more paranoid type, such that people believe that others are plotting against them. Most people who develop this condition respond to drug therapy.

Hallucinations

A hallucination is an experience in which individuals have a false sensation and perception but believe it to be real. Hallucinations may theoretically occur in any of the five senses, but more commonly they are either auditory or visual. Auditory hallucinations may take the form of people hearing commands being given to them to carry out certain things. Visual hallucinations, as I have discussed, may take the form of bizzare experiences in which animals, children, and so on are seen. Visual hallucinations tend to occur in organic disorders, such as acute confusional states, whereas auditory hallucinations are more often found in functional disorders such as schizophrenia. Auditory hallucinations may also be found in profoundly depressed people.

Management

Delusions and hallucinations may be treated with drugs. Sometimes these may be given by *depot injections,* in which case treatment may need to continue on a regular ongoing basis to prevent relapse. A depot injection is so called because the effects of some drugs used in treatment can last for some period of time after the injection is actually administered. One advantage of this is that people do not have to remember to take tablets regularly. However, it is worth noting that the development of more minor suspiciousness that falls short of being delusional may be more likely in people who live alone, are socially isolated, and have little sensory input due to very poor eyesight, hearing, or both. Psychological studies have shown that apparently normal people can develop these tendencies if subjected to long periods of sensory deprivation. Therefore, it is important to try to ensure that people receive adequate sensory and social input.

People with delusions, hallucinations, or both will obviously, by definition, have no insight into the fact that they are out of touch with reality, so it is unwise to confront them and insist that their experiences are imaginary. There may be instances in which they may be tactfully reassured that they are having these experiences because they are not well; however, if they are very restless and disturbed, this may be of little use, especially if they are also confused. Generally, arguments or situations in which strong emotions might be evoked should be avoided because this will make matters worse. A better option is to try to calm them down through reassurance that you are trying to help them and to show that you are listening to them, you understand what they are telling you, and you will do what you can to alleviate their discomfort. This is not to say that delusions should be agreed with but that they should be dealt with tactfully, straightforwardly, and in an honest way. At all costs, tricking them into a situation should be avoided, as should any attempt to say one thing and then do another or to be manipulative or false in approach because they will resent it later, and it will effectively hamper future attempts at help because of lack of trust.

The remainder of the disorders included in this chapter are usually classified as dementias and therefore might have been covered in chapter 4. However, because of their relative rareness (the exception being multiple sclerosis), they will not be encountered by many readers. For this reason I outline them briefly in this chapter instead. The psychological management approach is basically the same as that described earlier for dementia.

HUNTINGTON'S CHOREA

This was first described by Huntington in the 1870s. It occurs in approximately 5–6 people per 100,000 although this varies from one country to another. It is an inherited disorder—with a dominant gene being responsible—so that 50% of the offspring of parents who themselves have the disorder will inherit it. Unfortunately, though, preventing the disorder has proved difficult. The relatively later onset (i.e., middle age) means that there is the possibility of affected individuals having passed on the gene.

Initially, patients may present unsteadiness. A characteristic of the disorder is that individuals suffer a deterioration in personality and behavior in addition to involuntary movements. At first they may appear to be awkward and uncooperative, although their habits may deteriorate and they may become withdrawn. Paranoid ideas also frequently feature in the disorder. Management of these patients is often difficult because of this. The worst cases are often those starting at a relatively earlier age.

Unlike Alzheimer's disease, memory impairment does not feature predominantly in the early stages, but the intellectual deterioration develops gradually. The intellectual impairment tends to be global and is considered by most to represent an exaggerated aging effect. Insight and orientation are typically retained. However, patients with Huntington's chorea are often easily distracted, irritable, and prone to poor temper control. Depression and suicide attempts are not uncommon, and as already noted, patients often develop delusionary persecutory ideas.

In terms of brain damage, there is marked atrophy, and the bulk of the damage is to the frontal lobes. These areas are known to be involved in behavioral control.

CREUTZFELDT-JAKOB DISEASE

This is also a very rare form of dementia. It was described in the 1920s by Jakob and Creutzfeldt. Its main characteristic is that deterioration is very rapid. It is usually classified as a presenile dementia because it occurs more often in middle age. The cause is uncertain. It appears not be genetically inherited, but it has been proposed that a slow-acting virus may be responsible. The first symptoms reported by patients are typically tiredness and slowness, but they may also complain of difficulty in walking. Cognitive impairments tend to be widespread and include intellectual loss, memory deficits, and language problems. Patients may experience both hallucinations and delusions. The process, as already noted, is very rapid and death usually occurs within 2 years. As with other dementias, there is atrophy of the brain, although usually principally involving the frontal areas.

PARKINSON'S DISEASE

Parkinson's disease is one of the better known neurological disorders affecting elderly people. It was first described by Parkinson in the early 1800s. The characteristic features involve movement and include rigidity of muscles, slowness, and tremor. Unsteadiness tends to produce falls. There may be swallowing difficulties, constipation, and urinary incontinence. In a proportion of cases, there is intellectual and memory loss; this dementia is similar to that observed in Alzheimer's disease, although many patients remain intact cognitively. In others, there may be cognitive inefficiency caused by depression or medication rather than by the disorder itself. There is a high incidence of depression in patients. Mostly this seems environmental, which is to say that they develop a sense of hopelessness about the future because of the nature of the disorder. The age of onset is typically the mid-50s. The disorder may progress over a 10-year period, although often patients may not live that long, whereas in other cases patients may live for many years.

The cause of Parkinson's disease is loss of brain cells in an area called the *substantia nigra*. This leads to marked reduction of a chemical in the brain called *dopamine*. Therefore, treatment with drugs that will help to compensate for this (e.g., levodopa) is used. Many patients have been helped with this form of treatment, and life expectancy for them is better. During the last few years there have been a small number of experimental surgical operations in which certain types of cells have been inserted into the brains of Parkinson's disease patients. These cells have to come from a fetus. Because few of these operations have been conducted, it is not possible to draw any conclusions about the likelihood of this approach representing a breakthrough in treatment.

MULTIPLE SCLEROSIS

Multiple sclerosis is not a condition that occurs commonly in elderly people, with the usual age of onset being within the range of 20–40 years; however, the age of onset is occasionally later, and many patients will live into their 60s and will be found in nursing home environments. I therefore discuss it here briefly.

Multiple sclerosis occurs more often in women than men, with the sex ratio being about 1.4:1. It also seems to occur more in temperate than in tropical climates. It is one of the most common degenerative disorders of the central nervous system and the most common demyelinating disease (i.e., it is associated with the breakdown of the myelin sheath around the nerves). Initially, patients may present visual symptoms or movement problems. In the early stages the condition is characterized by alternating relapse and remission. Thus, the symptoms may occur and then abate for a period of time before recurring. The typical case follows this relapse–remit course, but some cases show a progressive deterioration. Eventually, however, most cases are characterized by progression with many handicaps so that patients may become paralyzed, incontinent, and have speech difficulties.

Many patients with multiple sclerosis are said to be euphoric in their mood, although this is now thought to be due to degeneration within the brain, especially to the frontal areas. However, depression is just as common and is probably due to the realization by patients that the future is not very bright. In advanced stages of the disease patients will show evidence of intellectual loss, problem-solving ability, and memory capability.

There is as yet little clear understanding of the cause of the disease. There may be a hereditary component and an environmental trigger. Like the dementias, there are no curative treatments. However, patients with multiple sclerosis do benefit from physiotherapy, and in other respects they should be managed in similar ways to patients with dementia.

WERNICKE-KORSAKOFF SYNDROME

Toward the end of the last century, Carl Wernicke noted a type of acute confusional state that occurred in some cases of chronic alcoholism. Some years later, another clinician named Sergei Korsakoff noted that in many cases these patients came out of this stage but developed permanent amnesia. The cause of Wernicke–Korsakoff syndrome is not in fact the direct effect of alcohol but rather of a thiamine deficiency. Indeed, there have been several cases described in which alcoholism was not apparent, but there was a physical problem that interfered with the absorption or metabolism of thiamine. The damage is to structures deep within the brain, especially to two areas: the thalamus and the mammillary bodies. The principal deficit in Wernicke–Korsakoff syndrome is the difficulty in learning new information, but their is usually a problem in recalling older memories acquired before the onset of the disorder, especially for the most recent ones. Sometimes Korsakoff patients will confabulate, which is to say that they will tend to fill in gaps in their memory with events that did not actually occur. This is not a deliberate attempt to cover up their deficiency or to fabricate but seems to be a genuine part of their memory deficit.

REFERENCES AND FURTHER READING

Lishman, W. A. (1985). *Organic psychiatry.* Oxford, England: Blackwell.

Martin, F. C. (1987). Diagnosis and management of acute confusional states. *Practitioner, 231,* 848–852.

7

Coping with Stress

Earlier in this book I made it clear that elderly people who are being cared for are not the only people who should be considered. Caring for disabled people is stressful. So far, I have addressed this only generally. For example, I have considered the importance of getting a break from caregiving. In an earlier chapter I looked at the nature of stress. In this chapter I examine the ways of managing it.

Three main levels of dealing with stress need to be considered: physical, cognitive (i.e., thoughts), and emotional. First, if you consider physical factors, you can identify certain needs that must be met. There should be adequate opportunity for sleep, exercise, relaxation, and nutrition. Stress is likely to be exacerbated by smoking, lack of exercise, too much caffeine or alcohol, and disturbed sleep pattern. I look more specifically at methods of relaxation in a moment, but general activities such as exercise, massage, swimming, or yoga will help to promote relaxation. Try to make sleeping regular and to avoid getting overtired. When you feel that your body is telling you it is tired, try to heed that warning. Allow a time every day when you can do a planned amount of exercise, such as going for a walk or a bicycle ride. Try to identify when you are wasting energy and learn to organize that energy better. Organizing a set plan and routine for the day or week ahead will help.

At the cognitive level, try to allow a time when you can be quiet, a time when you can think, and a time when you can plan. Organization of your time is a very important part of dealing with stress. Set for yourself realistic goals; nobody can exceed his or her capabilities, and stress is the price paid for trying to do so. Try to set aside a time when you can think about problems and avoid doing so at other times. If you find yourself thinking about problems outside of "problem time," try to focus your mind on other things that normally absorb you, such as TV, music, or some particular hobby or activity. Consider carefully whether you are doing too much, expecting too much, not taking breaks, or doing additional unnecessary work that either does not really need doing or that others could or should be doing. If there are several large jobs to be done, ensure that you work out a realistic schedule for doing them and avoid doing more than one thing at a time. Sometimes a good plan is to set aside, say, 5 minutes in every hour when you simply sit down and relax. In summary, then, make a routine for yourself and ensure that you keep to it.

Emotional and behavioral factors also need to be considered. You need to spend some time doing things you enjoy. You may need to assert yourself more and make it clear to others how you feel or what needs to change. It helps if you have a close relationship with someone who understands and who will listen to you. Social contact is important, as is the ability to share feelings and problems. Try not to do everything yourself if you can delegate some things to others. Another important thing is to reward yourself when you have achieved something. It does not matter how trivial that achievement may seem. Support from others may be gained by joining a club or society.

RELAXATION

It is a good plan to spend a part of each day practicing some kind of relaxation exercises. The following type of exercises take about 25–30 minutes to do, but do not rush because this obviously defeats the purpose of the exercise. When doing the exercises, try to ensure that you are in a quiet room by yourself at a time when you are not likely to be disturbed. You can do the exercises on a bed or in a comfortable chair. If you find that any particular exercise is uncomfortable or produces any pain, then leave it out. This could happen if, for example, you have arthritis that causes you discomfort. The exercises are divided into different body areas, so if you have a lot of tension in one particular area, then you can pay more attention to practicing the exercises for that area. For example, if you have a lot of tension in your neck and shoulders, or if you have frequent tension headaches, then spend more time on the exercises for the head and neck. If you experience frequent butterflies in your tummy or nausea, then spend more time on the exercises for the tummy muscles.

The first thing to do is to get comfortable. Spend a few moments concentrating on relaxing. Then take a deep breath, as deep as you can, hold it for a few moments, and then gently release it. Repeat this process of deep breathing for several minutes, and try to establish a comfortable rate of breathing in and out. Make sure that you are breathing from your diaphragm, using the capacity of your lungs and not just using the upper chest muscles. It is often easier to breathe in through your nose and out through your mouth, and when you breathe out, let the air release itself under its own pressure. A few minutes of deep breathing like this will help you start to relax. Breathing correctly is an essential part of relaxation, so it is important to ensure that you get it right.

Having spent a few minutes breathing deeply, the next stage is to carry out a number of progressive relaxation exercises. The easiest place to start is with your hands and arms.

First, clench your right fist as tightly as you can, hold the tension for about 5 seconds, and then relax it. Repeat the exercise, and as you relax notice the difference between the tension and relaxation. Also, you may notice that as you relax, your hand feels a little bit warmer. Now, tense your left fist, as tightly as you can, holding the tension for 5 seconds or so, and then relax. Again, repeat the exercise, noting the difference between the tension and relaxation. Next, clench both fists together tightly and then relax them. As you let the tension go, feel them become more relaxed. In between each exercise, just continue breathing deeply and slowly. Do not rush the exercises, but leave a gap of perhaps 5 or 10 seconds between each one.

Now concentrate on your lower arms. Hold both arms out straight and tighten the muscles in the lower parts of your arms. Hold the tension for about 5 seconds or so and then release it, feeling your arms relax as you do so. Repeat the exercise holding the muscles in your lower arms as tightly as possible and then gently relaxing. Feel your arms relax and continue breathing deeply and slowly.

Now move to the upper parts of your arms. Bend both arms and tighten the muscles in the upper parts as much as you can. Hold the tension and then gently release it. Tighten the muscles once again and then relax. Continue breathing slowly and deeply. Concentrate on your arms; feel them becoming more relaxed and try to let them relax further.

Now move your attention to your legs. First, tense your thighs by pressing your heels against the floor as hard as you can. Hold the tension for a few moments and then relax. After a few moments repeat the exercise. Continue concentrating on relaxing. Now press your heels down again, push your feet and toes away from your body, and tighten all of the muscles in your legs. Keep them tense for a few moments and then relax. Do that once again: Tighten all of the muscles in your legs and push your heels down and your feet and toes away from you. Relax once again and continue breathing deeply and slowly. For the next exercise, tighten the muscles in your legs again, press your heels downward, and pull your feet and toes in toward your body. Hold the tension for a few moments and then relax. Now repeat the exercise by pushing your heels downward, pull your toes and feet in toward the body, and tighten all of the muscles in your legs. Hold the tension for a few moments and then gently relax. Concentrate now on the increased feeling of relaxation in your legs and spend a minute or two trying to increase that relaxation still further.

Now focus on your stomach, chest, back, and shoulders. First, pull in your tummy muscles as tightly as you can and and hold them in for 5 seconds or so. Release the tension and feel your muscles relax. Breathe deeply and slowly for a moment or two and then repeat the exercise. Pull the muscles in and hold them tightly for a few moments. Relax. This time, do the opposite by pushing the muscles away from you and making your abdomen hard. Hold the tension and then release it. After a moment do the exercise again. Push your muscles away from you, hold your abdomen tight, and then relax. Spend a few moments concentrating on that feeling of relaxation in your tummy and try to increase it.

To relax your chest, take in a really deep breath. Hold it for 5 seconds or so and then gently let it out. Repeat this several times. Take in a deep breath, hold it for a few moments, and then let it go.

Now concentrate on your back. Arch your back by raising the middle of it, keeping your shoulders and lower part of your body flat on the bed. Hold it there for a short while and then relax. Feel your back relaxing. Now repeat that exercise by raising the middle part of your back, arching it, holding the tension there, and then relaxing it. Now spend a few moments concentrating on relaxing your back further and on spreading the relaxation across your back and shoulders.

After a few moments move your attention to your shoulders. Raise your shoulders, then lower them, move them forward and backward a few times, and then relax them. Continue breathing deeply and slowly, and then repeat. First, lift your shoulders, hold the tension for a few moments, release the tension, move your shoulders forward and backward a few times, and then finally relax and concentrate on developing the relaxation further.

Now, concentrating on your neck, move your neck to the right so that it moves down toward your right shoulder. Hold it there for a moment and then move it over to the left, down toward your left shoulder, and hold it there for a few seconds. Now move it back to the middle, move it forward down toward your chest, hold it there for a few moments, then move it backward toward your back, hold it there for a few seconds, and then relax it and bring it back to the middle. Now breathe deeply and slowly for a while and repeat the exercise. Move your neck to the right, pause, then to your left, pause, then forward, pause, then backward, pause, and finally bring it back to the middle and relax it as much as you can. After a few moments move your neck forward again and then turn it slowly round in a circular motion in one direction two or three times. Now do the same thing in the opposite direction. Finally, repeat this sequence by first turning your neck around in one direction and then in the other. Now relax completely and concentrate on relaxing your neck muscles as much as possible.

Concentrate now on your facial muscles. First, press your lips together and hold them like that for a few moments. Then relax them. Repeat the exercise by pressing your lips together once again and after a few moments relaxing them. Now tighten your tongue and push it against the roof of your mouth. Hold it there and then let it relax. Once again, tighten your tongue and push it against the roof of your mouth. After a few moments, let it go and feel your tongue relax. Next, clench your teeth together so that you can feel tension in your jaws. Keep them clenched for a few moments and then let the tension go. Again, repeat by clenching teeth together, holding the tension, and then letting it go and allowing your teeth to part slightly. For the next exercise, close your eyes tightly. Hold them tight and then relax. Now tighten them again and after a moment or two relax once more. Next, raise your eyebrows as high as you can and keep them that way for 5 seconds or so. Let them return to their original position and relax. Once again, raise your eyebrows, hold the tension, and relax. Finally, frown and hold your eyebrows down for a few moments. Then relax and let them go. Once more, frown and hold the tension, and let the tension go and relax.

Now concentrate on your whole body and try to relax further and further. Breathe deeply and slowly, in and out. Every time you breathe out, say to yourself "relax," and as you do so feel your body relax just a little bit more. Focus your attention on your arms and hands, and let them relax. After a few moments concentrate on your legs; let them relax further and become heavy. Move up to your tummy, chest, and back. Let all of the tension go and concentrate on relaxing more deeply. Relax your shoulders and neck, your jaws, mouth, tongue, lips, eyes, and forehead. The entire time breathe in and out deeply and slowly. Once more, focus on your hands and arms. Relax your hands, arms, legs, tummy, chest, back, shoulders, neck, jaws, tongue, lips, eyes, and forehead. Concentrate on relaxing more and more.

Now that you are relaxed, focus your mind on something pleasant—a place you would like to be or a thing you would like to be doing. You should make up your own image, but it might be something such as lying in the garden or on a beach, where it is quiet and peaceful. The sun is warm and you can feel its relaxing effect on you. It is quiet and peaceful, and you can just hear the gentle rhythmic background noise of the sea and the sound of birds singing in the distance. You can feel the gentle warm breeze on your face. You feel more and more relaxed as you let your mind concentrate on this image. Continue relaxing like this for as long as you want to. When you want to get up, just count backward from 5 to 1 slowly, and when you get to 1, just open your eyes. You will now feel pleasantly relaxed and rested.

Try to make the best of your relaxation by making sure you do not rapidly return to worrying and doing things. Make a conscious effort to try to maintain a reasonable level of relaxation. Ensure that you take your time to do things, that you do not find yourself doing too many things simultaneously, and that you continue to work to a well-planned schedule. Every so often ask yourself how tense or relaxed you are and rate yourself on a 10-point scale (10 = *extremely tense*, 0 = *completely relaxed*). Learn to recognize the difference between relaxation and tension, as well as what the signs for you are. You might be rushing around, breathing rapidly, having butterflies, and so on. Learn to stop and assess when you need to correct a rising level of tension. If you become aware of tension increasing again, take the time to sit down, just for a few moments, and do some deep-breathing exercises. Every time you breathe out, say to yourself "relax," and let your body go. Relaxation is much like any other skill. You will not become a master of it immediately, but if you keep persevering with the techniques, you will find that you can achieve more control over the tension in your body.

SLEEP

Sleeping difficulties are often encountered when people are suffering from stress. However, remember that people require less sleep as they get older and if they doze during the day. The relaxation exercises I just discussed should help if you do them in bed before going to sleep. However, there are some other possible methods that can be used. One such method is to try to do the opposite of what you are actually trying to do, which in this case means trying to stay awake. This may sound a little silly, but it is surprising how difficult it is to get to sleep if you actually try to do so. Sleep is one of those things that you have to let happen rather than make happen. You are more likely to fall asleep if you are bored or passively engage in something monotonous. One possibility, therefore, is to put all thoughts about going to sleep out of your mind. Instead, concentrate on thinking about something very tedious. Eventually, your mind will become unstimulated and you will fall asleep.

Some people always read or do a crossword puzzle before going to sleep. Such people find that this makes them tired, and if you are one of them, then this may help. On the other hand, if you find that this activates your mind, then it is best avoided. Above all, try not to think about sleeping or the consequences of not sleeping well; rather, learn to train your mind in relaxation skills.

ASSERTIVENESS

Stress is often made worse by lack of assertiveness. Assertiveness is commonly misunderstood as being either aggressive or selfish. However, it is different from either of these. When being aggressive we are normally being hostile, unpleasant, or unwelcoming. Selfishness implies that we are quite able to help another person but decline to do so for unacceptable reasons. Assertiveness, on the other hand, simply means expressing ourselves emotionally in an honest and straightforward manner: expressing anger when it is appropriate to be angry, being firm when we want to say no, crying when it is appropriate to cry, or saying that we love somebody when that is what we feel. Being assertive should not make us feel guilty; indeed, people are more likely to respect us if we do assert ourselves.

Part of being assertive comes from setting limits, as I have already discussed in the chapters on stroke and dementia. We can help others to a point, but not beyond that point, and within the limits we set. If someone demands something of us that we know to be unreasonable or beyond our capabilities, then it is appropriate to be assertive. Many people feel guilty about saying no, but if the limits are clearly communicated from the outset, later problems can be largely avoided because people will recognize when, how much, or even if we can help them. This is not putting ourselves before others or being selfish but merely being realistic. If stretched beyond our limits, we ourselves will suffer stress and will be of no use to anyone, as I have stated previously.

Being assertive means not using phrases such as "I'm sorry" unnecessarily or "I'm afraid" inappropriately, but saying "I should like" or "Please would you," and so on. It is simply a question of stating the fact of how we feel and what we think in an appropriate manner. If we fail to assert ourselves at the time, then later we will frequently regret it, feel angry or tense, or get angry with the wrong person. An example might be that somebody telephones us, we agree to do something, but then later realize that that was not the right thing to do or that the request was unreasonable. We may then resent this and react inappropriately, or a member of our family may get angry because he or she was not consulted. At the time when such an unreasonable request is made of us, our bodies normally alert us to the fact—we feel uncomfortable or tense. This is a sign that things are not quite right, and we should then try to focus on being assertive at the time. Rehearsing or role-playing situations with another person is a good way of practicing assertiveness skills.

There are different ways in which we can say no, depending on the circumstances. Sometimes it may be appropriate to say something such as, "Unfortunately, I am unable to do it" and to repeat this if the questioner persists. In other situations it may be appropriate to explain why we have to say no: "Unfortunately, I am not able to help today because of an alternative commitment." On other occasions we may wish to add our concern: "I know that you would like my help this morning, but unfortunately I cannot do it." It may be appropriate to offer some alternative, such as "I cannot do it today, perhaps tomorrow" or "Is there an alternative time?" Remember that sometimes it may be necessary to repeat your assertive response if the questioner is persistent, as may happen in a dialogue with a salesperson. Just keep saying no.

However, being assertive does not just mean saying no. It means being able to express your feelings clearly and without feeling awkward. This means paying compliments appropriately and simply.

Another feature of assertiveness is expressing anger when this is appropriate. Failing to express anger can lead to this being expressed in an inappropriate manner: getting angry with the wrong person, throwing objects around, sulking, being uncooperative, and so on. It may be represented in other ways, such as in headaches, anxiety, and tension.

Learn to recognize when you are repressing anger and when it is later expressed inappropriately, and learn to express yourself in a more assertive manner.

REFERENCES AND FURTHER READING

Fontana, D. (1989). *Managing stress.* London: Routledge & British Psychological Society.

Marks, I. M. (1978). *Living with fear.* London: McGraw-Hill.

Mills, J. W. (1982). *Coping with stress. A guide to living.* Chichester, England: Wiley.

8

Death and Bereavement

Death is a topic that is seldom discussed in our society despite the fact that we all have to face the experience, at one time or the other, of people close to us dying. It is perhaps understandable enough that it is an avoided topic of conversation, but as a result, many people probably do not really know what to do or have probably never thought about what to do when someone dies. The purpose of this chapter is to outline the things that do need to be done and then to look at the bereavement process. First, I briefly discuss dying.

DYING

In these days of relative longevity, the most likely causes of death are heart disease, cancers, and respiratory disorders. Men can expect to live about 70 years; women do better, averaging 76 years. Yet, at the turn of the century, people would have done well to live past their late 40s.

Of course, many people die naturally, as it were. However, in other cases, there may have been a long illness. Few terminally ill people are ever told about the gravity of their condition, perhaps because of the awareness that being told that one has a fatal illness may lead to grief and denial. Despite this, though, most people state that they would wish to be informed if they have a terminal illness; in fact, many do realize that they are dying. Relatives, on the other hand, are usually made aware of the fact. There is an obvious problem with this situation: Because neither the relative nor the person dying knows what the other knows, no discussion about the matter takes place, and it may be only at the last moment at the bedside that this can be done. Therefore, this period is often likely to be stressful.

When people are dying it is not unreasonable to try to fulfill their wishes—to talk about their impending death if that is what they wish, to help them retain their dignity, and to help them to die as painlessly and comfortably as possible. This requires treating them as being normal and as "living" and in a way that is as fulfilling as possible.

Good general care is very important in terminal illness, for bereavement will be less painful if the symptoms have been well controlled. All of the general aspects of caregiver outlined earlier need to be given: making them as comfortable as possible, preventing pressure sores, attending to hygiene needs and self-care, and providing medication to reduce or prevent pain. It is important because, as has been the general tone of this book, although some additional care may be required, the basic needs of people are the same regardless of their physical or mental condition. A special need of terminally ill people may be pain relief. Sadly, it happens far too often that medication for pain control is given reluctantly or prescribed "as required." There is, however, no good reason why medication should not be administered at regular intervals and that sufficient dosage be given. For example, although some of the painkillers likely to be used are addictive, this is hardly important if someone is dying. If necessary, medication may be administered continuously by subcutaneous infusion.

People who are dying may have fears of several things,

and these things may need to be discussed. Such fears may include pain, the process of dying and of the state of death itself, being a burden on others, becoming decrepit in appearance, losing control of bodily functions, and worrying about how relatives will cope after their departure. It hardly needs stating that anxiety and depression are commonly experienced by terminally ill people and their relatives and that these symptoms may exacerbate any experience of pain. Anxiety tends to be more common in those with a longer terminal illness and will persist because of the uncertainties ahead; although there may be a need for anti-anxiety medication, much can be achieved through discussion of the feared situations, by the provision of good basic care, and by general support. However, remember that most terminally ill people do not suffer severe degrees of anxiety and depression. Most people do not die under traumatic conditions but do so relatively peacefully and painlessly. This is how we should all wish to die, and it is our responsibility to ensure that, as much as possible, this is how things will be.

THINGS TO DO WHEN SOMEONE DIES

For a person who dies at home, it is necessary to call the doctor to issue a death certificate. In the case of a person who has asked for cremation, the doctor will need to obtain a signature from a second doctor. If the person dies in the hospital, then the death certificate will be signed by the doctor who is in charge of the person's care.

The next stage is more difficult because it will be necessary to inform relatives and friends who will obviously be upset, especially if the death has been very unexpected. It is also difficult because of one's own feelings of despair.

When the death certificate has been issued, arrangements will need to be made with a funeral director. The person's body may be left at home or taken to a funeral home. Burial or cremation arrangements may then proceed. The coffin may be taken to the church either from home or from the funeral home and will be placed in front of the altar. The service itself will obviously be a very emotional moment because it signifies the finality, but comfort will be derived from the presence of relatives and friends. The burial or cremation then proceeds.

BEREAVEMENT

Death, as I have said, is little talked about in our society. Initially, we are confronted with the finality, with the knowledge that this is it and that we will never see or speak to that person again. It is that permanent loss that makes facing the death of a friend or a relative difficult. A person may move out of our lives for a while, perhaps years, but there is always the knowledge that he or she will return or that somehow this is possible even if improbable. But with death there may have been things left unsaid, apologies to be made, feelings to be expressed, forgiveness to be asked for, and so on. For some, the inevitable grief is worse than for others, but the grief is normal and should not be avoided. The emotions should be expressed and the tears not held back. By grieving it is possible to come to terms with the death and to readjust to life. Life is not the same, and in the early stages, readjustment may seem impossible or too far off to see.

The process of bereavement has been divided into various stages, but these blur into one another considerably and, from a practical point of view, cannot necessarily be separated from each other. The very first reaction is denial. Sometimes it is aptly referred to as a feeling of numbness. Outwardly, the bereaved person may appear calm and able to cope, or stunned and apparently unable to comprehend the situation, in which case support and care from others may be required. It is a normal reaction that defends us from the suddenness of the blow. We find ourselves thinking that perhaps it is not real, that we are dreaming, that a mistake has been made, that somehow it is not really happening. This stage may last up to a few days, but varies from person to person. It is replaced with anger. The emptiness, silence, and absence will be constant reminders of the reality of the loss. The practicalities of having to deal with the funeral arrangements help us through these early days. It is common to "see" the loved one or to feel that he or she is still there or to expect him or her to walk in at any moment. Periods of grief are likely to be worse at times when the person would normally have been there. The bereaved wife may find the evenings and weekends worse. Anger may be expressed at others who may be seen to have failed in their duty. God may be blamed for taking the loved one away and letting the person down. Attempts may be made to bargain with God to bring the dead person back. This phase may continue for a few weeks, and it then gives way to a more prolonged stage of depression. There may be the experience of guilt and self-blame. Symptoms of anxiety and depression will occur periodically and may be quite severe. Panic attacks may be experienced, and these, although gradually decreasing in frequency, may continue during the first year. By now the things that had to be done have been done, people stop calling, and one may be left alone to face the loss. There may be feelings that there was something that could have been done or should have been done, or that one has been negligent in some way. The person may become restless, unable to attend to things, wandering around aimlessly and searching for something to do. Work may be turned to overactively as if in an attempt to avoid the grief. Places where the lost person once used to spend time may be visited. A sort of identification with the dead person may occur, so that, for example, the symptoms that the dead person once had are experienced by the living person. This stage is marked by a prolonged depression that may become deep, with poor sleep and appetite, and if very severe may require professional help or treatment. However, only a minority may be distressed enough to require this; it is very important to see bereavement not as an illness but as a normal process. Thoughts about the lost one tend to be obsessive, painful though they are, and difficult to keep out of mind. This phase marks the beginning of the recovery phase, with the repeated experiences of grief somehow acting as a gradual desensitization. Recovery is well underway when the periods between the spells of acute grief become longer and there are periods without the overwhelming grief. The readjustment process may now begin. Reaching the summit of this long hill may take 2 years or more, maybe less for others, but it does not come quickly or suddenly; it would be difficult to specify a time when one can say one is finally over it. It is a gradual adjustment process through which one establishes a new independence, a new identity. In the end there will be happy memories, but the bereaved person will gradually become more detached from the painful emotions that once accompanied him or her.

COPING WITH BEREAVEMENT

It is often advised that when possible, as in cases in which a person is suffering from a terminal illness and death is anticipated, that some preparation takes place. Hopefully, the family will be able to look at the future realistically, make plans, and grieve together.

Even those who are not particularly religious may derive great help spiritually, especially during the bargaining and depressed phases. It will also help to have a person who can listen empathically without criticizing or reacting emotionally to the expression of feelings and anger.

It should be appreciated that experiencing the stages of bereavement is normal, that the person may feel alone, and that the event of the death of a loved one has an effect that is not temporary. The process of adjustment is a continuous one, and it is difficult to isolate an exact point at which one has achieved this. Anniversaries will be more difficult times and should be anticipated and again recognized as normal.

When trying to help the bereaved person, it is important to take a sympathetic approach, showing genuine interest and understanding. Problems of denial or nonacceptance should be dealt with by gently getting the person to be more realistic. Particularly if the person is alone, he or she should be strongly encouraged to develop or resume social contact, for this is important in making a good adjustment. Crying should not be avoided because the expression of grief is also important in the process of acceptance. In other cultures death and bereavement are dealt with collectively. In the Jewish culture, for example, 3 days are given to deep grief, followed by 7 days of mourning, during which there is self-disclosure, getting together with others, and talking about feelings. Mourning is done openly and there are prayers. This is followed by 30 days for gradual readjustment and then a period of 11 months for rememberance and healing. The advantage of this system is that it not only encourages but also facilitates self-disclosure.

The widow or widower will now have to make certain decisions about the best thing to do for the future. One such decision may be about whether to stay in the same house or to move, perhaps to live with another relative. However, it should be recognized that some time should be allowed to give oneself the chance to adapt to living alone first before rushing into making what could turn out to be a wrong decision or one that is later regretted. There may be financial restraints or other considerations; it is sometimes useful to list the positive and negative aspects of moving and other major decisions.

Bereavement is likely to be more difficult in certain situations. These include situations in which (a) the death was just one of several closely occurring life events; (b) the death was sudden or unexpected, especially for younger people; and (c) the relationship was unusually close, ambivalent, or dependent. Young women who lose their husbands are likely to have more difficulties, as are those who were previously more susceptible to depression. Older people are less likely to have adaptation problems. There seems to be little doubt that positive religious beliefs are helpful because they assist in the provision of support; similarly, people will be helped if they have a supportive social network. In other words, those who are well adjusted psychologically and socially before the death will adapt better. However, remember that here I am talking only of average reactions and that at the end of the day every individual will respond differently.

CONCLUSION

The purpose of this book has not been to give the impression that caring for elderly people is an easy task. Indeed, it is not, and there are no simple or quick solutions to the various problems encountered. However, much can be achieved just by being more aware of what the problems are, understanding their nature and, where known, their cause and the ways of tackling them. Of course, it is difficult to do this in more than a general way. It is not possible to predict what problems will be encountered, and the same method of dealing with them will not work on all occasions or with all people. Inevitably readers will find their own solutions, but often knowing that one is taking the right approach is reassuring in itself. However, no book can be a substitute for personal support and practical help. At the risk of repeating it once more, it is important to meet this need by getting into contact with the relevant professionals, organizations, and volunteer organizations.

REFERENCES AND FURTHER READING

Hinton, J. M. (1972). *Dying.* Harmondsworth, England: Penguin Books.

Parkes, C. M. (1972). *Bereavement: Studies of grief in adult life.* London: Tavistock.

Ross, E. K. (1970). *On Death and dying.* London: Tavistock.

Index